From God in Person,

Master Fard Muhammad

HOW TO
EAT
TO LIVE

Book One

BY
ELIJAH MUHAMMAD
Messenger of Allah

Published by
Muhammad's Temple of Islam No. 2
7351 South Stony Island Avenue
Chicago, Illinois 60649

Books by Elijah Muhammad

MESSAGE TO THE BLACKMAN IN AMERICA

HOW TO EAT TO LIVE

CONTENTS

CONTENTS

Right Way to Eat

There is no way for us to learn the right way to eat in order to live a long life, except through the guidance and teachings of Allah, Who came in the Person of Master Fard Muhammad.

The Bible says that He will give us more life abundancy, but He demands strict obedience to His Will. There is no way of prolonging the life of human beings — or any other life — unless it begins with restrictions of the foods which sustain life; the right kinds of food and the proper time when it should be taken into our bodies.

Jehovah taught Israel how to live, but Israel rebelled against the law of Jehovah, handed down to them through Moses, the servant of Jehovah.

There are many Jews today, called Orthodox Jews, who try to eat in order to live. They are careful of the type of food that goes into their stomachs. They will not slaughter an animal without trying to drain that animal's blood out of its body before taking it for food. They will not accept diseased animals, birds or fowls.

We give credit to the Jews for still trying to obey that which they were ordered to do by Allah, through the prophets that Allah sent to them. The Jews paid the penalty for disobedience, and are still paying. However, they are the only people, the Holy Qur-an teaches, whose food we can eat. They, in turn, can eat our food. The Muslims who try to live according to the teachings of the Holy Qur-an will not eat the wrong food when they know what that food is.

Of course, those who are becoming converts to

1

Islam in America. my followers. are being tried The Christians — white and black — try to force or deceive my followers into eating foods they know we, the Muslims, do not approve.

In prison, they almost starve my followers trying to force them to eat the filthy, poisonous swine flesh. This I know, because when I was in prison they did the same to me.

Thanks to the coming of Allah in the Person of Master Fard Muhammad, if we obey what He has given to us in the way of proper foods and the proper time to partake of these foods, we will never be sick, or have to pay hundreds, thousands and millions of dollars for doctor bills and hospitalization.

The Christian people have one of the most brutal ways of killing animals for their food. Many of their animals are killed under fright and excitement; they actually murder the animals they eat.

We, the Muslims, who have not been able to go out to the slaughter houses as yet to choose our meat, as the Orthodox Jews are doing, slaughter our animals or cattle at a time when they least expect it. We take their lives in the name of Allah, with a prayer over this condemned life to be used to sustain our lives.

Allah has taught me how to eat in order to live. I have been teaching it to my followers, but we often become negligent and fall victim to our own negligence. As a result, we are calling the doctor. or going to the hospital because we did not eat the right foods, and in the proper way.

Hereafter, I shall enforce restriction on my

2

followers to eat as Allah bids us. As I have said to my followers on many occasions, life cannot be prolonged unless we are careful of what we eat, and when we eat.

The foolish idea of eating three or four times a day — and all between meals — is like the poisonous swine who never has any regular eating habit. Even a dog will not eat when he is full most of the time. The hog, however, swallows as long as he can, and then regrets that he can't keep swallowing. He will crawl into his food and wait until he can swallow some more. He is so greedy he won't leave his food.

Vegetables

Virtually all vegetables are good to eat except collard greens and turnip salad. The roots of turnips do very well, but not the salad. Cabbages are good, especially the white head, but not the green leaves. Cauliflower is a really fine vegetable, but take away the green leaves. There are a lot of other good vegetables that have been grafted from original vegetables, though some of the grafted vegetables are not good to eat. Do not eat the vegetable called kale.

Eat some spinach, but do not become an habitual spinach eater. Eat rutabaga — a little every now and then. You may eat as much garlic and onion as you like, but no sweet potatoes and no white potatoes. Sweet potatoes were never good for any human to eat. They are good for hogs, but not for you. White (Irish) potatoes are a food for people who live in frigid zones — a staple food for such as Europe, Northern America and Canada — but potatoes and rice are too starchy for you and me. They laden us with too much starch and fat, which are friends to diabetes. Sweet potatoes are full of gas; do not eat them. There are many more vegetables you will find edible or forbidden to eat in this book. If you like, write me for information on other vegetables not mentioned here.

PEAS

Allah forbids us to eat peas. He considers most peas fit for cattle and herds of animals, but not for the delicate stomachs of human beings. No black-eyed peas, field peas, speckled peas, red peas or brown peas. Do not eat the split peas you find in the store.

Peas, collard greens, turnip greens, sweet potatoes and white potatoes are very cheaply raised foods. The Southern slave masters used them to feed the slaves, and still advise the consumption of them. Most white people of the middle and upper class do not eat this lot of cheap food, which is unfit for human consumption.

BEANS (DRY)

No beans did He advise, except the small navy — the small size and not the larger size — the little brown pink ones, and the white ones. This bean He valued to be very high in protein, fats and starches, and it is a safe food for prolonging life. As you will find, most of the Muslims like their bean soup. These beans are dry beans. He said that He could take one of our babies and start him off eating the dry small navy bean soup, and make that child live 240 years. He described no other bean. This dry bean, or pulse, is of ancient origin. It was this bean, according to certain historians, that Daniel preferred for himself and his followers in the prison of Nebuchadnezzar. Do not add rice and meats to these beans, because they contain proteins, fats and starches.

FRUITS

Virtually all fruits are good. We eat apples, oranges, bananas, pears, peaches, tangerines, mangos, plums, grapes (do not eat processed dried grapes, eat natural sun dried grapes), pomegranates, lemons and grapefruit.

BREAD

Eat whole wheat, but not the whole grain — it is too much for the digestive system. Eat wheat — never white flour, which has been robbed of all its natural vitamins and proteins sold separately as cereals. You know, as well as I, that the white race is a commercializing people and they do not worry about the lives they jeopardize so long as the dollar is safe. You might find yourself eating death, if you follow them.

He flatly forbids us to eat corn bread. The white race, and some African people, used to live off corn bread, because it is cheaply made. It is not good for human consumption because of its potency, which only animals stomachs are able to digest. Positively do not eat corn bread. If you must, or are forced to eat it, He said to cook it two or three times, put it up, sour it with a good yeast, dice onions into it, and let it ferment like wheat bread. After this, cook it two or three times.

Never eat fresh, hot corn muffins, or hot cakes and syrup. When you eat half cooked bread, it shortens your life, as all bread will rise again in our stomachs, buckling our stomach and intestinal walls. The more it is cooked, the less this will happen.

Rye bread if it is cooked enough is fine to eat. It is not good for office people; they are not active enough to digest such a bread. It is good for a working man doing manual labor. Office workers should not even eat baked beans, nor beans with rice and meat in them because their jobs do not permit them enough activity to digest such heavy foods.

Prepare Your Own Food

Take time and prepare your own foods. Do not kill yourselves by running to the store buying processed foods to eat — and never buy those ready-made biscuits.

We plan to install health food departments in our bakeries, grocery store, and restaurant soon. Watch for them.

Do not eat the highly rich soy bean, which is a new flour on the market. These beans are for cattle not human beings. The oil from soy beans is not good for our stomachs. Soy bean flour is being mixed with wheat flour by the flour mills. In fact, the Christians are experimenting with all foods. They do not care what they eat as long as it does not kill them instantly. Beware!

For good health, we should raise and prepare our own food. As I said in this book, the white race is a commercializing race by nature. It is the almighty dollar they are after, not long life.

Remember, cook your bread thoroughly. Make thin rolls, so that you can cook them well done. The rolls should be sliced, and those slices of bread should be toasted through and through before they are eaten. There is no such thing as being too stale. Actually, stale bread is better on your stomach and digestive system. Positively eat no nuts.

The eating regulations in this book are a "must" with my followers. Begin at once — eat only one meal a day, regardless of the work you are doing.

Do not put lard in your bread. Use vegetable oil, corn oil, pure butter, olive oil, or whatever good vegetable oil you choose. Keep any hog, or swine, out of your foods. Do not eat fried or hard -baked foods, if you can avoid them. When it comes to meats — no fried chicken or steaks; nothing fried. Fried foods are hard on your digestive system and will cut short your life.

Food God Suggests

What food does Allah (God) suggest? He suggests the food that is good for us and does not make us ill — food that is for human consumption and not for animals.

Never before have we gone so far astray. The European white race, blessed with the privilege of eating the best food the earth provides, has taught us to eat the worst (divinely prohibited) food. We eat all the time, three and four times a day. This is enough to wear out the intestines of a brass monkey.

Eat a single meal a day, no matter what anyone says. If your doctor says that you should eat more than one meal a day, ignore him with a smile, and eat only once a day. If he tells you he eats three meals a day, tell him that his length of life is about the same as his patients. Then, tell the doctor to try eating one meal a day.

The more idle our stomachs are, the longer they will last. The more we tax our stomach, the sooner it wears out. We all try to live as long as we can, because nature never teaches us that we should not try to live. We do not have a nature that teaches us to die, or teaches of life somewhere else.

No matter how staunch a believer the Christian may be in a life after the grave, if he gets sick, he sends for the doctor. He prays to stay on here and not to go to the unknown.

To live a long time, Allah, in the Person of Master Fard Muhammad, has taught me life must begin with the type of food that will prolong life. We have been talking about bread. There are people so poor they

9

have no choice, and there are some so rich who still have no choice.

Whole wheat bread, cooked thoroughly, is the best bread. It should be ground very fine. It can be ground almost as fine as its white kernel. Never eat corn bread. As I said, rye bread is all right for the hard-working man. Even at that, it should be cooked twice.

The Christian civilization has taught the so-called Negro slave to eat freshly baked bread, white biscuits or white rolls, just out of the oven, and it scorns old bread, which is better for the stomach than freshly baked bread or cakes.

There are many foods we would like to teach you not to eat, but at present so many of you cannot avoid eating them.

We must prepare and grow our own food, because this is a highly-commercialized world. They graft a lot of food, and some of this food is not good for our stomachs.

Soy bean flour is very rich, and not good for our stomachs. Our stomachs are too delicate for soy bean flour — therefore, leave those beans alone. The animals, especially cattle and hogs, love them. Grind them up and they will eat them. They are very high in protein. The lima bean is another large bean advertised by the devil for you to eat, which will almost burst the lining of the stomach and intestines of a Texas bull. They said "that one is good for the nigger." Do not eat the smaller ones, either — the ones they call "baby lima beans" (baby belly busters).

Pastries and cakes — the kind made with crusts of

white flour and sweetened with white sugar, so sweet you can still taste them the next day — are not good for our stomachs. All this hastens you to the graveyard sooner than you would like to go. We should eat fruit and fruit pies. I love that little black blueberry pie — huckleberry, as we call it in the South. But do not make it with white sugar or crusts of white flour. Use brown sugar and whole wheat flour for your pie and cobbler crusts.

Apples are better when eaten raw than when made into pies. This goes for pears, peaches and bananas. All fruit is better for you raw than cooked. When fruit is raw, we get the benefit of its natural vitamins. If possible, never eat cooked fruit.

If you must eat meat, always eat the cleanest, such as healthy and tuberculosis-free beef. The lamb is the best. Most beef is too coarse for our stomachs. The lamb is a much finer-grained meat.

Eat small young pigeons (squabs) which have never flown from their nests. Do not eat any bird that has been free to fly around and look for its own food. This is the teaching of Allah to me. Chickens are not fit to eat. You have to nurse them so carefully to keep them away from filth.

If you would like to find good food, such as lamb, beef or even chicken — if you are a Muslim — buy it from the strictly Orthodox Jew. Be certain it is an Orthodox kosher market, because some Jews eat the pig. Orthodox Jews are excellent in protecting their health, even spiritually trying to do and eat like their prophet Mossa (Moses) taught them through the Divine teachings of Allah. If you respect yourselves as

Muslims, the spiritual Orthodox Jew will respect you. Of course, no one will respect you unless you respect yourself.

Do not eat ground meat, unless you see it ground.

Do not buy the Christians' ready-prepared ground meats, or any ready-ground meat. Buy the quality meats that you like, and have them ground by the Orthodox kosher butchers, through their meat grinders, because they do not have the pig near their shops. They are like us — they hate the divinely-prohibited flesh.

If you must eat rice, please brown it thoroughly in your oven or on top of your stove with a little butter or oil to keep it from sticking. Keep stirring it vigorously. Remember, eat only one meal, once every 24 hours.

Why They Urge You to Eat The Swine

The taking of the prohibited flesh of the swine as a food is beyond righteous imagination. It is difficult to understand why Christians eat such divinely-prohibited flesh, while having a Bible and the law given to Moses against the swine flesh. Other prophets, down to Muhammad, preached against the eating of the swine.

Christians are among the largest consumers of pork in America, and they deliver this rat throughout the world to other people. They are so fond of swine flesh that they sacrifice it in the church, and then ask divine blessing upon it. They barbecue and cook it, and hold a feast in their places of worship and eat this slow-death poisonous animal — which God has forbidden — as though they had an option with God.

No wonder Isaiah says that they stand behind one tree in the garden, eating swine flesh, the abomination, the mouse and the broth of the swine in their vessels. And yet, they will tell all the Muslims and Orthodox Jews that they are holier than we who don't dare even to touch the swine's carcass.

Preachers and priests are working along with the enemy, or adversary, of God, teaching the people that it is all right to eat swine — their bellies stretched with the hog in them and saturated with the whiskey and wine. This is the type of religion under which you have been brought — Christianity and its preachers and priests. None of them have tried to prevent you from breaking this divine law by teaching you the consequences of such an act.

Allah taught me that this grafted animal was made for medical purposes — not for a food for the people — and that this animal destroys the beautiful appearance of its eaters. It takes away the shyness of those who eat this brazen flesh. Nature did not give the hog anything like shyness.

Take a look at their immoral dress and actions; their worship of filthy songs and dances that an uncivilized animal or savage human being of the jungle cannot even imitate. Yet, average black people who want to be loved by their enemies, regardless of what God thinks of them, have gone to the extreme in trying to imitate the children of their slave masters in all of their wickedness, filthiness and evil.

The Arabic meaning of hog, or swine, according to one Arab Muslim, is Khanzier. Khan, he says, means "I see." Zier means "foul." This is the meaning of the English word swine. Khanzier, or "I see the animal foul" — and very foul — is the best explanation that I have heard to cover the very nature and characteristics of this animal.

He is the foulest animal. He lives off nothing but filth. The only way you can get him to live and eat better food is to keep him from getting to filth. He is so poisonous (99.9 per cent) that you can hardly poison him with other poison. You can even give him lye — something you'd think would cut up the intestines when eaten.

Snakes can't poison hogs; they eat them and fatten.

The bite of snakes doesn't harm them, because they eat the biter. He is so poisonous and filthy, that nature had to prepare him a sewer line and you may find the opening on his forelegs. It is a little hole out of which oozes pus. This is the filth of his body that cannot be passed fast enough.

His poison is that of a live nature, in the form of a parasitic worm that is called trichina (commonly known as pork worm), which is found in the stomach and intestinal walls — until it finally breeds and works itself into the muscles of the body of the eater. From there, the trichinae work themselves into the spinal cord and travel the spinal cord toward the brain, at which time there is no possible cure.

They then cause the victim to suffer with rheumatism, backaches, stomach aches, headaches, fever — and even change the color of the eyes of some eaters to a dull brown or dull red. They fill the eater with a drowsiness, laziness — slow thinking, slow moving and the tendency to be easily irritated. The swine eaters are always ready to rise up for a dispute and fight other people and among themselves.

He is the greediest animal. He never knows or cares to stop eating, as long as he sees something to eat. He is the dumbest animal. He keeps his nose smelling and eyes looking for something in the earth. You could feed him all day long, and he will never look up to see his feeder.

In the case of bad weather, arising, he is never intelligent enough to go in before it actually starts raining or hailing on his back. He takes no warning. He will keep his head in the earth, rooting until the storm is lashing his back with rain and the lightning is blinding his eyes.

You eat this animal from his snout to his tail, and all of the poisonous wormy intestines. Yet you say you are holier than any religious people.

Please learn to eat one meal a day — and let it be without swine flesh. And many of the ailments that you are now suffering and getting medicine from the doctor for, will disappear.

To you diabetics: Eat one meal a day and lay off that starch and sugar. They are only making you sick.

Write and let me know that you have tried eating once a day, shunning sugar and starches, and before a week's time, your urine will be negative of sugar and acid negative.

It is ignorant for you to suffer with this disease, when it can easily be cured — just stop eating that which is causing your trouble. Eat one meal a day. You will not starve and die.

The Pig: Swine

I think we have said enough about the poisonous animal called, in Arabic, Khanzier. Beyond a shadow of a doubt the swine is the filthiest and foulest animal human beings could have resorted to for food. The flesh of the swine, while cooking, has a very different smell from that of other animal's flesh while cooking. And even when it is not being cooked, it has a bad smell.

Worms and insects take to its flesh while in the farmer's curing stage faster than to any other animal's flesh. And in a few days, it is full of worms.

In many cases, the eater of the flesh becomes nauseated when the flesh is being cooked in the early morning. It is a divinely proibited flesh, and God (Allah) has prohibited you and me, my brothers and sisters of the Black Nation, from eating it or even touching its dead carcass.

Please, for our health's sake, stop eating it; for our beauty's sake, stop eating it; for our obedience to God and His laws against this flesh, stop eating it; for a longer life, stop eating it and for the sake of modesty, stop eating it.

Do you know that if we, the 22 million lost-found members of our nation here in America, would stop eating this pig (his poison swine flesh), it would mean a great economic saving to us? And I do not think the government would be so eager to eat it themselves if we would obey this Divine law against this divinely-prohibited flesh. There is an old, foolish answer our people have given to such advice:

"The white folks eat it, and my grandparents ate it, and they lived to be 75 and 80 years old."

If Noah and Methuselah had heard you boasting that your parents lived only 75 or 80 years eating poison, they would have considered your parents as never having grown up to become adults, according to their good way of eating the best food, about twice a week, and living nearly 1,000 of our present calendar years which consists of 365 days.

God does not punish us for the crime of disobedience to His laws when we are ignorant of His laws. But after knowledge of His laws, He is justified in punishing us by setting the full penalty according to the disobedience.

As I have previously said in this book, most vegetables that are sold on the public market are good to eat with the exception of those Allah prohibits; such as collard greens and the rough turnip salads. You have plenty of other vegetables to eat. And you have good beans other than lima beans, field butter beans (called baby lima beans), and black -eyed peas (field peas as we call them.)

Fasting

Fasting is a greater cure of our ills — both mental and physical — than all of the drugs of the earth combined into one bottle or a billion bottles. Allah (God), in the Person of Master Fard Muhammad, has taught me that fasting, with the right kind of food, is the cure for our ills. He has said to me that there is no cure in drugs and medicine. And this the world is now learning. We can take medicine all of our lives until it kills us (yet, we are still ailing with the same old diseases).

The bad foods and drinks that we are putting into our bodies keep us a victim to illness. There are very few nice doctors who like to tell you that drugs are not good for you, because they paid for their learning and want to keep practicing. But "How to Eat to Live" is what we want to know and have wanted to know all of our lives.

All men and women want to know how they can prolong their lives. Nature teaches us to stay here in this life as long as we can.

Nature has never taught anyone that he should leave this life and find another one somewhere else, because we only have one life. And, if this life is destroyed, we would have a hard time trying to get more life; it is impossible. So try to keep this life that you have as long as possible. Go when you cannot stay here any longer.

Allah taught me that one meal a day would keep us here for a long time; we would live over 100 years. Eating one meal every two days would lengthen our lives just that much longer. He said to me that you would never be sick, eating one meal every three days.

The fact that fasting is the cure for 90 per cent of our ills is known by the medical scientists. But, they do not teach you that. They know that tobacco, hard whiskey and alcohol are not good for you and will shorten your life and kill you.

But, most of them are too weak themselves to stop drinking, smoking or chewing tobacco. So they do not teach you that tobacco and alcoholic drinks made into what is known as whiskey, beer and wine are not good for you, although they know it to be true. They will say, "Yes, it is good for you if you are temperate." But they know that once you get started on that stuff, it is such an enemy that it just takes you into its power and it is almost like trying to break an iron chain to get away from the habit. So, do not use tobacco in any form and you will live a few years longer.

Fast once a month for three days, four days, or for whatever length of time you are able to go without food without harming yourself, and you will feel good. Did you know that if you would stop eating pig and the food that you should not eat, stop eating three and four times a day and stop drinking whiskey, beer, and wine, you would save much in the way of money?

In prolonging your life by abstaining from the pig, alcoholic drinks and tobacco, you will also be adding money to your savings by hundreds and thousands of dollars. You will be depriving those pig raisers, tobacco growers and alcoholic distillers of millions of dollars of which they rob you as they hasten you to your grave.

You could stop the tobacco growers from growing that stinking weed by turning away from the use of it. And you could stop the pig raising by not eating the stinking hog. These things are death to your children in their early ages. They even affect the reproductive organs of people in the early ages, as well as affect the heart, lungs and your sharpness in thinking. And, after all of this, you die a victim of poison and commercialization.

LEARN TO EAT TO LIVE.

One Meal A Day

Eat one meal a day or one meal every other day, and it will prolong your life. Do not think that you will starve. On the contrary, you will be treating yourself to life, and a life filled with sickless days. You can hardly get sick eating this way. I know because I have this experience. If you eat the proper food — which I have given to you from Allah (in the Person of Master Fard Muhammad to Whom be praise forever) in this book — you will hardly ever have a headache.

In eating once a day or once every other day, you must not eat between meals. And, you should try to eat at the same hour tomorrow as you eat today. Do not change your meal hours if you can help it. That causes your stomach to react to various hours of the day for a meal, and will set up gas on the stomach. Do not even drink juices, milk, or soft drinks between meals.

And, do not eat candies or fruits between meals. You are welcome to drink water, but I know you will not want too much water between meals since your stomach will not call for it. You may drink coffee between meals, but do not fill your cup with half sugar and half cream and pour coffee on top of that. (smile) This (that I am trying to teach you) is the way that He (Almighty Allah) has taught me for you. I have given to you in this book the type of food that you should eat as Allah has given it to me.

Again I say, many vegetables are good to eat; also many fruits. But the vegetables you have been warned against eating — such as collard greens, turnip salads, black -eyed peas, field peas, lima beans, butter beans and soy beans — should not be eaten. Be sure that you do not eat the large -size navy bean; eat the small size navy bean.

Surely sugar diabetes can be controlled and driven out with your abstinence from eating sugar and starchy foods. And, with your corrected way of eating once a day or once every day (if started in time), you will become negative of sugar in your blood. If you are a victim of sugar diabetes, you should not eat white or sweet potatoes. And even if you are not a victim of diabetes, you should not eat too much of any starchy food (such as potatoes) — and positively no sweet potatoes. You should be careful of eating this type of food.

Beware of starchy Foods and Sweets

God Almighty has taught me — and many others — that we should never eat more than one meal a day. That will most certainly heal you of many complaints. Since the American citizens eat more meat, sugar and starchy foods than they should, there is almost an epidemic of too much sugar accumulating in our blood. Eating one meal a day, which does not include too much sugar, will keep you healthy, both physically and mentally, if you are a Muslim believer in Allah and the religion of peace (Islam).

I warn all you sufferers of diabetes to stop eating starchy foods and sweets until this disease vanishes out of your blood or cannot do you any harm. If you eat once every other day, it is almost a guarantee that you will not be sick.

The Orthodox Jews are a people who have lived among us in Asia, and they still try to follow Moses' teachings on how to eat to live. The Holy Qur-an teaches us that we can eat their food and they can eat our (the Muslims) food, because the two people (Jews and Muslims) try to eat the right food to live. I have learned, and most likely you have too, that it is only a weakness of ours to eat constantly. We are only digging our own graves with our appetites and teeth. There is no teaching from anyone — God, you, or me — that will help us if we take our appetites for our guides.

Within one week you can get used to eating once a day, and within one week you can get used to eating once every other day. Many of the Muslims are eating like this, and you can eat this way too. Our stomachs are just the way we train them to be. Get away from those fattening sweet pies two or three times a day. And do not eat those white potatoes at every meal; they are full of starch. Do not eat fresh bread, and you should never eat white bread because it is the worst bread you can eat and it will shorten your life. In fact, you should not eat too much fattening food. You are not going to get weak.

Eat plenty of vegetables and fruit. Eat meat? If so, eat clean, fresh meat whether it is beef, lamb or chicken. Do not eat too much of it. Change sometimes, and have fish for your meal. Many of our people like to eat young pigeons (squabs), but usually they are a little too expensive.

Do not eat too much of anything — good or bad food — and do not eat but once a day. You will soon tell me how much better you feel. Do not smoke or use tobacco in any form or way and do not eat the pig even if you have to starve to death.

How Allah's Way Prolongs life

Many are advertising what to eat, and what medicines to take to make you eat or stop you from eating. Many books are written and sold on good and bad foods, as well as on reducing the weight and on how to increase the weight, introducing the many chemicals used to bring about the desired result. But Allah, in the Person of Master Fard Muhammad, to Whom praises are due forever, has given us a better and safer way to do these things.

His way will prolong our lives and do away with our sicknesses. And, that way is eating one meal a day — or if we are able and do not have too much physical work to do, eating one meal every two days. This alone will prolong your life.

You will not be sick often if you eat once a day and eat the proper food. The proper food is that food which is not poisonous. The slave masters taught us to eat the rough foods, such as field peas, and today, being accustomed to eating them, we still eat them along with sweet potatoes (which are not good for anyone but hogs) and white potatoes (which, since they are so starchy and fattening, are not good for anyone unless they are in a zone where they cannot secure better food).

We cannot live a long time if we laden our bodies with fats to burden our hearts in pumping blood through all of this fat. It shortens the time of our heart beat, and the fat person is — in many instances more likely to attract sickness and disease.

Why are we healthier and our lives prolonged by eating as God has taught us in the Person of Master

Fard Muhammad, to Whom praises are due forever? It is because of the one meal a day or fasting. Eating once a day and fasting gives the body time to rest from the previous meal and to absord it properly and distribute it where the body is calling for it.

Some of us eat so often and so much at a time that it actually has a tendency to make us small and skinny because we never allow time for the previous meal to digest and distribute the vitamins and proteins into the proper places and throughout our bloodstream. Rest, given to the digestive system of our bodies, is the thing that prolongs our lives.

In this period of rest (24 hours), the poisons that we ate in the previous meal are not capable of doing us any harm (when it is minor food poison), for the idleness of the stomach destroys this poison that would upset us or shorten our lives to a great extent. Therefore, we live a longer life if we eat correctly and do not eat three meals a day. Only one meal a day is sufficient for adults no matter what their occupation may be.

Milk and bread (wheat bread) alone will keep us alive indefinitely, and it is the best and the most easily digested food. We have plenty of supplements for milk and bread, so eat them, but eat them only once a day. This will reduce your doctor bill almost 90 per cent, and if you eat once every two days, you will not have any doctor bills. So, do not tell the doctor that I told you this. (smile)

As you know, I contracted bronchial-asthma, and I have learned that there are no drugs that the public has access to which actually serve as a cure. But I am doing fine now, and eating once a day and once every other day does ·not give the mucous time to accumulate and choke the bronchial tubes and tract.

All praises are due to Master Fard Muhammad, as it is written of Him in the Scriptures, that He comes to prolong our lives and to do away with sickness and death. If we live right, He teaches us we will enjoy life for a long, long time.

How to Keep Food From Hurting Us

I thank Allah in the Person of Master Fard Muhammad, to Whom praises are due forever, for bringing to us life and light so that we may be able to enjoy life, and to enjoy that life longer than we have previously enjoyed it.

Many years could be added to our lives if we only knew how to protect our lives from their enemies. As He (meaning Master Fard Muhammad) said to me, food keeps us here; it is essential that we eat food which gives and maintains life. That same food destroys life Therefore, to keep this food from destroying our lives, we must protect our lives as well as we possibly can from the destruction of food. If we eat the proper food, and eat at the proper time, the food will keep us living a long, long time.

Eating three and four times a day is to your stomach as dripping water is to a stone or iron. The dripping water will eventually wear the stone and iron away. But, just to look at the water, it does not appear powerful enough in its dripping to wear the stone and iron away. It is the same with food; we continuously put it into our stomachs to be digested and eventually it will destroy the stomach. If we let our stomachs rest a while and gain strength, they will last longer in doing a job of digesting food for us.

Eat one meal a day and eat the food that will not harm you so quickly. You do not have to obtain a long, detailed knowledge of what foods you have to eat, because the wrong food has already been pointed out to you — foods such as the pig, nuts, white flour, meats (of course, we eat some meats), the wrong kinds of peas, the wrong kinds of breads, too many starchy foods, and too many sweets.

All of these foods destroy us. Bread should be cooked thoroughly and slowly, and if you have plenty of time, cook the bread two or three times and then eat it. Meat should also be cooked two or three times.

Eating great meals of highly seasoned and sugared pastries is definitely not good for us. They most surely will take years of our lives away. You may eat some sweets, but do not make an entire meal of sweets or eat them every day. Fruit is good for us; we should eat plenty of fruit.

To live a long time, eat once every 24 hours or once every 48 hours, if you are able to do so. But, if you have heavy, manual work to do, do not try to eat once every two or three days. And, if you eat once a day, you should fast every month for two or three days. By doing that, there will be no poison left in the body at the end of a year to make you sick even one hour.

I would like you, who try to live and eat just as this book teaches you, to please send me a letter telling me of the results that you have gained from eating as I have instructed you in this book. I repeatedly teach that the way Allah, in the Person of Master Fard Muhammad, has taught us to eat will do away with many doctor bills and do away with much maiming of the limbs caused by certain diseases.

Sugar diabetes can be controlled and cured if you only eat correctly. Stay off sugar and starchy foods and leave those old, white potatoes alone. Do not eat spaghetti and macaroni at every meal. If you are over

- weight, do not eat it at any meal, and if you want to live a long time, do not eat it at any meal. Foods such as spaghetti and macaroni are processed, not cooked thoroughly, and are hard to digest.

There are some people who claim that they do not receive beneficial results as they should. This is due to wrong mental food that they are eating, which has an effect on their digestive system. To get good results from eating the proper foods, we must have good thoughts.

The Proper Food
and The Proper Time to Eat It

Eating the proper food that has been given to us and taught to us by our God and Saviour, Master Fard Muhammad (to Whom praises are due forever), changes us in many ways. Not only does it give us good health, but it gives us a better way of thinking, as food and our mental power work in the same way. Whatever affects one, affects the other. Eating the proper food also brings about a better surface appearance. Our features are beautified by the health that the body now enjoys from the eating of proper food and also eating at the proper time.

Bad food takes away even the beauty appearance of a person. God taught me that the swine (hog) takes away three one-hundredths per cent of the beauty appearance of a person. This we can easily understand and see after we stop eating it. The medical scientists also will agree with us that the poisonous flesh of the hog will take away three one-hundredths per cent of your beauty appearance.

There are some people who have eaten so much of this ugly, poisonous animal—and he is the ugliest and silliest-acting animal you have ever looked upon and been around, as well as the filthiest animal that you have ever dealt with — that they actually look like that animal. It is a divinely-prohibited flesh. It is a sin for you to eat it.

The enemy of God (the devil) teaches you to eat it, and he eats it himself to show you how little respect he has for God's divine law against eating this prohibited flesh.

He drinks all of the intoxicating drinks, offers them to us, and then preaches the same gospel in the church that "Thou shall not eat the pig. Thou shall not drink intoxicating liquor. Thou shall not rob, steal, murder, commit adultery, gamble, hate, and lie to one another." Yet, he is doing that hourly. Everything that God says "Thou shall not do" in the Ten Commandments given to Moses, they say thou shall do.

It was only a waste of God's time to have given this race of evil people good guidance, because it is just as Jesus said in a parable, "The wicked husband who was given overlord of the earth and its people, never did offer the true owner any of the heir (a convert of righteousness)."

We have nothing to fear or worry about in the way of right guidance today, because we have God Himself in Person with us to lead and guide us in the way of truth and righteousness.

There is a lot of difference in the beauty of true Muslims and that of Christians. I do not mean to say that there are no beautiful Christians or Black people who eat the hog. But, there is a difference in their appearance of beauty that can easily be discovered by one who obeys this divinely - prohibited law against eating swine flesh. The poisonous hog flesh makes the color of many people's eyes muddy and reddish in appearance and makes the people who eat it brazen, careless, easy to anger, fight, and oppose each other.

Eat the proper food as given in this book and eat at the proper time; one meal a day from 4 to 6 P.M.

The Right Food and The Proper Time to Eat It Is Becoming a "Must"

To live without sickness and without fear of a short span of life is now a must for the people who expect to see the Hereafter. The way that God, in the Person of Master Fard Muhammad (to Whom praises are due forever), is teaching us (the lost-found members of the aboriginal nation) is the best way; regardless of what it is. Whether it concerns food, mental stability, or what have you, He teaches us in the best way.

I offer you His teachings, and it is up to you to accept or reject them. But, I repeat, His is the best way as He says in His Holy Qur-an, "I Allah am the Best Knower" (Chapter 2, verse 1). Since He represents Himself as the Best Knower, then it is nothing but intelligence on our part to follow and obey that Best Knower Who gives the best advice and Whose guidance is best for our future regardless of what we desire. He is the best Knower of what guidance we should have.

There are many disbelievers, infidels, and atheists today as the Bible teaches: the fool has said in his heart that there is no God. These ignorant sayings and attacks made against truth go for nothing today but condemnation with truth. (We do not have the type of God that they were taught of: some spook God and man. But, there are supreme men among man and this Supreme One is referred to as God, having infinite wisdom and knowledge over all things.)

There will be no sickness or disease among us when we learn and obey the law of nature. The law of nature is the divine law the Creator set for us in the beginning of the creation of the universe. This race (white) of people has ignored and disobeyed this law and has met with disaster. They seek, and have tried throughout their civilization, to change the very natural religion of the black man.

But, time has proved that the white man was a failure and now has met his unnatural and false teachings and practices with truth and reality of the law of nature and its workings among the created creatures of God. This law is now to defend us against the false guidance and rebelling of this race (white).

Let the white man eat all the hog he wants. It was made for him, not for us. It was made for a cure for many of their diseases and is used for salves.

If you want to enjoy good health, eat only once a day and nothing between meals if you are not sick. There is an allowance made for the sick ones who, sometimes, are not able to eat enough at one meal to take them over to the next meal, or whose bodies are weak and must be built up for the one meal a day. In this case, they sometimes eat two meals a day, but never three.

If you can eat one meal every other day, you will enjoy both health and a longer life. Even the men and women who do strenuous mental work can go along with one meal a day if they eat the proper food and never want more than that.

Fruit Is Digested Better
When Eaten Raw

Since being given knowledge by the All-Wise One in the Person of Master Fard Muhammad on "How To Eat To Live," we should not confuse ourselves by studying the advice of all the people, doctors, and quacks of the world on what kind of medicine, vegetables, meats, herbs, and fruits we should eat. If we keep getting advice on the above after getting the correct advice, we will never enjoy good health. All will be confusion.

As I mentioned earlier, nearly all vegetables are good to eat that have been classified by the scientists who have studied the poisons that the vegetables contain as well as the non-poisons they contain. We do not need to eat everything just because the Bible (in Genesis) said that Adam (who represents the white race) could eat nearly all of the herbs of the earth (that are not poisonous). Our scientists teach us of that which is poisonous and of that which is not poisonous.

If we are travelers and are stranded, we eat whatever we can find edible, to non-poisonous roots and the bark off trees. But this is not good for us if we wish to live a long time because our stomachs are not made to digest the bark off trees and roots of trees or blades of grass and leaves.

Our stomachs were not made to live off raw foods, except certain raw foods such as fruits, which—beyond a shadow of a doubt—should be eaten raw and never cooked. When we cook fruit, it takes away the vital property that is necessary for our good health. An apple (or peaches or berries) is better eaten raw than cooked, unless our health and body are weak and unable to digest the raw apple.

There is a great need for knowledge on what to cook as well as how to cook it. We can live a long, great and healthy life by just drinking good, wholesome milk and eating good whole wheat bread if the bread is cooked correctly.

Some people will eat whole wheat kernel. But, this is not good to do because it is the hull of the seed and our stomachs are not made to digest the raw wheat seeds, regardless of the great property of vitamins in them.

The whole wheat kernel should be milled and ground very fine. When you are ready to make bread, add water and yeast to it and set it aside to sour. This will put it in a better digestive state to be cooked properly for your stomach to digest.

Cook it slowly after it has risen a couple of times in the mold; this must be done thoroughly so that all of the risen cake or loaf is thoroughly cooked through and through under the heat of the oven. After it is cooked, do not eat it until it has set a day or two; even three days is not too long to wait for it. It is never stale because of age if kept in the right place.

Never eat freshly cooked bread of any kind, as it is difficult for the stomach to digest. The same applies to beans and whatever you eat; cook them thoroughly. But, do not cook them in such a way as to destroy the vitamins or proteins that are in them to strengthen and build your bodies and the tissues of your bodies.

Some people pull the brown crust off the bread to eat the unbrowned core. But by doing this you are throwing away the most digestible part of the bread and accepting that part which is hard to digest.

Toast that is browned through and through is much easier on our stomachs than the slice of bread that is not toasted. We can live longer by eating several varieties of foods.

Never think that you are a great, healthy person just because you eat a lot of meat, white bread, corn bread, sweet pastry, or a lot of peas and beans. You are only taking a quick trip to the cemetery.

Overindulgence, The Enemy

Yes, a quick trip to the cemetery if we indulge in too much of anything. It becomes an enemy to us. Remember at all times when you are eating that you are to live and not to die. As I said previously in this book, white bread and corn bread are not good for our stomachs to digest. Regardless of how many hundreds and thousands of people eat this before you three times a day, it is still not the food for you and me to eat if we wish to live a long and healthy life.

America's people consume more sweets than any other people on earth. They love their sweet, fat pies, cookies and cakes at every meal. America has more bitter trouble with her health. Eating too many sweets piles up sugar in the blood and it becomes the enemy of our lives. Our blood is our life.

Just think of the way we destroy our lives by eating too many sweets or two much meat; or eating white bread and corn bread. Ask yourself that question.

America is a great candy seller. She reaps a harvest of wealth on just selling sweet candies and nuts. They fill the candy full of nuts, as well as their cakes, cookies, and other pastries. The only thing with stomach enough to digest nuts is an animal. Birds love nuts and they have what it takes to digest them. Nature made them that way.

Just as horses can digest corn and anything else in their line of food, birds, squirrels, hogs, coons, rabbits and worms can digest nuts. They can eat nuts and digest them and they will not wear out their stomachs like yours would wear out trying to digest them.

A dog's stomach and his digestive juices are like any carnivorous eating animal's. He can digest a rare steak. In fact, he can digest it as soon as he kills the animal. You do not have to cook their food. They do not like it cooked; they like their meat raw. That is the way nature made them—to take it raw.

People (like the white people) who love dogs and other animals, change their way of eating so that it is against the very nature in which they were created to eat. You cannot make him a member of your family by seating him at the table, to eat good, cooked food. He will live off it, but it is not the way nature made him to eat.

Try offering him some raw meat and cooked meat. He will eat the raw meat before he will eat the cooked meat. Offer a cat a piece of raw fish and a piece of cooked fish and see which she will eat first. Raw foods appeal to their appetites as cooked food appeals to ours, but we can eat both.

It is very dangerous for you (whose civilization is not limited, but is limited if you follow the limited ones) to follow a civilization made by nature for a short time in their ways. This is what we have been doing, and this is what we must stop doing if we expect to survive.

There are hundreds of drug stores throughout the country into which we should not go for anything except first-aid if we hurt ourselves down the street or road somewhere; not for something to stop aches and pains in our stomachs caused by eating the wrong food. We should not call the doctor for such foolish and ignorant mistakes as eating the wrong food and eating it too often. We should be ashamed to call the doctor for these errors.

Eating the wrong food and eating it too often starts trouble in the physical body everywhere — from the sole of your feet to the crown of your head. As I said, you do not have to eat everything that people say is good to eat. It is a fool who does that. You do not need everything that is good to eat to live a happy life. Take some of those things that are good to eat. Of course, you should have a balanced diet. I certainly agree with you there.

There are several ways you can prepare your meat and bread that will give you a sharp appetite at every meal if you prepare it differently. Bread can be cooked two or three times and also meat. It is best for our stomachs and our longevity.

They both should be cooked twice before eating. Of course, they will not look as fancy as when they are freshly cooked, because the more you cook them, the more the surface beauty fades away. But the more permanent your life will be and that good old stomach will last a long, long time if you allow it to rest after a hearty meal, no matter how good the meal was or how easily digested.

Give your stomach from 24 to 36 hours to rest to digest its food. And, if you can take 48 hours or 72 hours, that is fine. But first try 24 hours and then 48 hours next. Do not try to start with 48 and 72 hours.

Get used to eating one meal a day, then when your appetite is not so strong for that next meal, by eating once every 24 hours, start eating every 48 hours. Never start 72 hours regularly until you are able to do so.

Some of us have started eating every 48 to 72 hours

and have to change back to one meal a day. This is not good to do. Fast 72 hours every now and then while you are eating once every day, (if you want to), once a month or once every two or three months.

Never eat more than one meal a day unless you are sick and unable to eat the proper food due to the weakness of the body to carry you over 24 hours.

Our Big Problem
Is Eating Too Much and Too Often

I repeat, the main thing in "How to Eat to Live" is to eat only once a day or once every other day. This will take care of everything. You cannot go all over the earth trying to eat everything that people say is good to eat. But give what you do eat time to get out of the way for the next meal and the effect that it probably would cause. Brothers and sisters, let your stomachs rest. Stop trying to eat three meals a day and all in between. That is enough to kill chickens and hogs.

Anyone who eats all the time has a very short life. Our greatest trouble, when it comes to sickness, is due to staying at the table, eating too much and too often. You have no regularity about your eating at all.

"Eat any time," they will tell you. One of the gravest wrongs you could do is to eat when you do not want to. They say behind that, "Eat before you get hungry," which is one of the silliest things of all.

If your stomachs are not asking you for food, please, brothers and sisters, do not put any in. The stomach will let you know. Wait until you are really hungry. Do not act like a pig and want food every time you see it.

Nature did not make the hog and bird with any regularity in eating. Although hogs will stop eating when they get enough, the foolish pig will never stop eating until he is sick and all but ready to drop dead. The horse will stop eating and the house cat will stop eating when it has enough, but people will not. It is just as the old saying goes, "We dig our own graves with our teeth."

We drive many impurities out of our bloodstream if we do not fill our stomachs with food two and three times a day. Some Christians never fast until their doctor tells them to do so. They know nothing about stopping their eating for even one day, let alone for over three or four days.

The majority of them are afraid to miss even a single meal. They think they will be sick from missing a meal. This is very ignorant. A dog will stop eating if he gets sick, but not some people. The doctors have to force them to stop eating so that their medicines can give good results.

Your main trouble is eating too often and eating the wrong kinds of food. Time and again I have warned you against eating that rotten, stinking pig with millions of worms in his flesh. He is the ugliest and most stinking animal. Even his house and everything about him stinks. If you cook him, he stinks. With his ugly, muddy, reddish eyes, his ugly mouth, and his ugly ears, he is just ugly. He is the silliest and most brazen animal.

The devil certainly did a 100 per cent job in turning the people against everything that God said "Thou Shall Not Do." He has made the words say in works, "I shall do." Allah said that these ugly animals (the pig) take away your beauty appearance.

Live right, think right, eat right, and do right. You will not have to die to go to heaven to be like angels; you will be like them while you live.

Why and How We Fast in December

I have chosen (for quite a few years) the month of December for my followers to fast as in the month of Ramadan. It serves as a sign that we (the Lost and Found Nation) are the end of all signs pertaining to the pilgrimage and fasting in the month of Ramadan.

We fast the 12th month of the Christian year to relieve ourselves of having once worshipped that month as the month in which Jesus was born. It is now known and agreed upon by the scholars and scientists of religion that nothing of the kind took place 2,000 years ago. Jesus was born, not in the month of December, but rather — as God has revealed it and according to the season that history claims existed in that time — the first or second week in September.

The Christians have made holidays which are used mostly for commercialization. They buy wine, whiskey and beer and fatten up pigs and hogs for the kill and roast this divinely-prohibited flesh to celebrate what the Christians call the birthday of the Son of Man. Jesus condemned such things as drunkenness and the eating of swine flesh.

The act that they carry on for the celebration of Jesus' birth is perfect for Nimrod, who actually was born on the 25th of December, according to the scientists and historians, as well as the words of God, Himself, spoken to me.

Nimrod was an enemy of God and one who came in the last 300 years of the 2,000 years of Moses. He led the white man against the laws of Moses and the worship of Allah. He (Nimrod) wanted them to worship idols and that which was other than God (as they did in ancient Rome).

Let us, my followers, remember the right way. Waste not your earnings in such ways as worshipping and feasting as the Christians do. They only say and do not. They have taken for themselves the profit of God and the place of God.

In this month of fasting we shall keep our minds and hearts clean, and we shall not indulge in the eating of meats (land meats). You may eat fish and such fat products which come from land animals such as butter and cheese.

In this month, we should keep our minds on Allah, Who came in the Person of Master Fard Muhammad; my God and your God and my Saviour and Deliverer and your Saviour and Deliverer to Whom be praises forever for giving us life after our mental death for the past 400 years.

During this month, eat before day and after the sun goes down (if you wish) but not during the daylight hours. This also goes for drinking; drink whatever you are going to drink either before dawn or after dark. The eating before dawn is for those of us who love to eat breakfast in the mornings. But if you eat one meal a day, you may eat that meal either before dawn or after dark. It is better for your health, however, to eat one meal after dark.

Keep up prayer, and let us all be grateful to Allah for His coming in the Person of Master Fard Muhammad throughout the month of December and every month. And during this month, let there be no quarreling or disputing in our homes or abroad.

The Food and Its Eater

Neither I nor you can thank Almighty God Allah, in the Person of Master Fard Muhammad, enough for going after the very mainspring of life; that which everyone loves to keep as long as he possibly can. Even animals, beasts, insects, fowls of the air, and fish of the sea want to keep their lives. And, I do not care how good a Christian you are, or how much you would love to see Jesus, or how much you would like to go to Heaven to see Jesus and to sit down beside him, as the Christians teach you will do (smile), you never make any preparations to hurry to go out of this life to find another life.

The very law of nature teaches us to hold on to this life and not let it go if we can help it. We only know of this life and not any other life. You strong Christians and lovers of life beyond the grave — and life somewhere in the skies that you imagine — never prove to anyone that you would like to leave this life for that life by killing yourself or telling the doctor not to come to administer medicine or any aid that he can give you when death is approaching.

Whenever death approaches, you want it to go back and let you stay. In view of that, the best thing to do is to try to preserve and keep this life that we have and know as long as we can and go when we cannot stay here.

The only way that we can have life, keep life and prolong life, is by what we eat and how often we eat it. This is the way of life. The Bible teaches us that God will prolong the lives of the righteous. But, there is no God Who can prolong our lives without checking on what we eat and how often we eat it.

We must not be confused, I repeat, with the various advice offered to us from the modern-day food and medical scientists. If you take their advice and try to eat all of the different kinds of food, cooked in their many different ways, at all different times of the day, and their many different suggestions on how much you should eat, you will most certainly die. Brother and sisters, I repeat: it will most certainly kill you — with the exception of the Orthodox Jews' food, which is good.

According to the history of the white man by Almighty God Allah, in the Person of Master Fard Muhammad, to Whom praises are due forever for His life-giving words, teachings and guidance of us, the Lost and Found members of the aboriginal black nation, the white man began eating meat. They had no stoves and cooking utensils as they had today, when they were driven into the confines of the hills and cavesides of Europe. They ate animal food, beast food, and whatever they could get of flesh to eat. This race with all of its modern, scientific knowledge of how to grow food and receive the best food the earth produces, are still great flesh eaters.

They have taught the world of man to eat as they eat. Their medical scientists have learned that meat hastens and destroys the life of man. But, they practice eating the very worst meat (the poisonous and filthy swine, wild birds, wild fowl of any kind, and even reptiles) and teach man to eat it. To follow them in everything they eat and drink means that you are absolutely inviting death. Even to seafood, they drag out in their nets the very scavengers of the water and advise you to eat it because they eat it.

We must remember that this race is conscious that they are not to live on this earth for very long. Therefore, eating poisonous food and drink and eating three and four times a day, will take you along with them very fast. This is the secret knowledge of the death that they caused us to suffer through foods.

The poor, blind, deaf and dumb Lost and Found so-called Negro will eat and drink anything he sees his white master eat and drink. But, I want you to stop doing this ignorant thing and eat the right food that you will find in this book. And, eat only once a day. I do not care what kind of work you are doing, eat only one good meal a day.

If your work is light office work or light housework, you could eat once every other day if you wanted to without any hindrance. Once you get used to it, your stomach will only ask for a meal at the time that you have trained it to eat.

In regard to you who suffer from sugar diabetes, fasting and staying away from sugar and starchy foods is far better than having your limbs cut off your body because of your foolish carelessness in eating sweets and starchy foods all times of the day. Cut out that sugar; do not use any at all. Use honey, but not the whole bottle full at one time. If you have too much sugar in your blood, be careful not to eat any sugar of any kind until you get it out.

Some doctors will tell you that you have low sugar.

But just tell them that you will have "high life" in you. Do not eat any potatoes, beans, and bread. Eat vegetables. You may eat chicken if it is raised away from filth.

There are poultry raisers who raise chickens in clean places and give them good food such as corn, oats and other little grains that are not harmful to the chicken or to us. They also give them bread and milk. You do not have to fear eating chickens like these. But, if you can do without eating any kind of flesh, that is fine.

Whole milk that is clear of TB germs is best for us to drink. But, if we cannot get whole milk, we can drink the milk that the dairies have but we should boil it at a certain temperature in order to kill that probable germ.

Drink plenty of milk and eat butter instead of so much of this artificial butter made of vegetable fat, and you will have better health.

Food Can Be Life or Death

We can shorten and destroy our lives by the way we prepare and cook the food we eat. Allah, in the Person of Master Fard Muhammad, to whom praises are due forever, taught me that all of our food (not including fruits) should be cooked, and cooked until thoroughly done. And it should be seasoned with salt, where necessary.

The food we eat should not be poisonous food, such as the flesh of swine and of wild animals, birds and beasts. We should not eat fish that weighs more than 50 pounds, water scavengers in the form of the fish family, and other water animals of that kind.

As we know, there is much animal life taken as food from water today that we should not eat. The believers of Islam should be aware and not eat such foods.

In cooking your food, be sure that you cook it thoroughly, but not to the point where it loses its taste. Safeguard your delicate stomach that has to digest all that you eat by not over-burdening it with trying to digest half-cooked food or raw food and the acid gases from such foods. This is what hastens the doctor to your bedside — and after that, the undertaker, and after that, the grave digger.

Remember, we kill ourselves by what we eat and how we eat it. Just as food is our source of life, it is also our source of death, as God has taught me. Food keeps us here and it takes us away. For long life, take long intervals between your meals, and do not eat over one meal a day.

How to Live More Than 100 Years

Allah (God) has taught me, in the Person of Master Fard Muhammad, how to eat to live, so that I also may teach you. He desires to extend our lives from a short span, averaging 62 years, to a span of one thousand (1,000) years — or for as long as we desire to live. He said there is no set time for us to die. We kill ourselves daily by means of what we think, what we eat and what we drink.

Think about it, and you will agree that we kill ourselves. As I said in an earlier chapter "How to Eat To Live," there is no way of prolonging life except by being careful: watching and examining what we put into our bodies to sustain life, and the regularity of our eating and drinking habits. We have been taught what to eat and what to drink by a people (the white race) who has never obeyed the law or religion of Allah (God).

These rules Allah (God) gave Moses' people in the Ten Commandments for their good — clear as a mirror: law and guidance, which they should not forget. However, they kept none of this. Everything that Allah said "Thou shalt not do" they have ignored and said "Thou Shalt Do." Therefore, the Christian race is no example or guide for one who seeks to obey the law of Allah (God) for God now threatens to remove them from the planet earth. If they would stop deceiving the people, making them believe they are what they are not, and trying to change the natural religion of Allah (God) into the unnatural, which is false, their doom probably could be delayed.

There is a sect among them whose members call themselves Orthodox Jews (a few who still try to follow the Ten Commandments given to them through Moses). These are wiser, more skillful, than the Christians.

How to Eat to Live? Allah (God) said to me, in the Person of Master Fard Muhammad (to Whom praise is due forever) that we who believe in Him as our God and Saviour should eat but one meal a day (once every 24 hours). Eat nothing between meals, not even candy, fruit, or anything which would start the stomach, digestive processes. In this way, our eating of the proper foods and drinks — at the proper time — would extend our life to 140 years. This would protect us from sickness.

He said if we would start our infants eating one meal a day, as soon as they are able to partake of solid foods, it would enable them to live to an age of 240 years.

I then asked Him, "How about eating once every 48 hours?" He said to me, "You would be ill only one day out of four or five years."

I asked Him what was the cure for that one day of illness? He said "Fast three days and you will be all right." I asked Him, "What about eating one meal every three days?" He said "You will never be sick if you eat once every 72 hours. ' This is about two meals every six days, which would extend our lives to a span of 1,000 years — for there is no poison from the previous meal three days ago which has enough power to do you any harm. The fast destroys the accumulation of food poison.

The body is made up of water, chemicals, stone, metals, vegetation and air. All that is in the earth is, in some form, in our bodies, and you have no birth record of the earth. Although there is a record, you probably do not have it. It is a very old earth. It is not — as you have been made to believe — only 6,000 years old. It is more than six trillion years old, and it will be here for a long, long time yet.

What comes out of it, such as life, cannot live as long as the earth itself. But it can be made to live a very long time if carefully nursed, according to its nature, as you see and scientists teach you the long life of the California Redwood tree (sequoia sempervirens). There is mentioned in the Bible of Allah (God) a saying that His people's life will be as the tree. There is an oak in Arabia — under which they claim Abraham met God — that is still alive today. Allah (God) never intended that righteous lives should be cut short of 100 years on this earth.

I have experience in living and eating according to the way He taught me for a while and I found it one of the happiest and most peaceful ways of which I ever dreamed. I began with eating one meal a day and forced my family to do the same for several years, until I was picked up and sent to prison for teaching Islam in 1942. Of course, the government said they sent me up for failing to register. That really was not the reason, for I did not come under the draft law at that time. Some of my followers, 60 65 years old, were sent to prison at the same time. Persons of such an age were not desired by the War Department.

While in prison, the Christians made it hard for us to live as we had been. They deliberately put swine, or the essence of the swine, in everything and the

assistant warden made mock of it when I told him my
followers lived on nothing but bread to avoid swine.
He said that even the bread had swine in it. We used to
make a meal of dry, baked white potatoes. We had it
hard — and all my followers now in prison still have
it hard. All those converted to Islam in prison at
present suffer in order to avoid eating the divinely -
prohibited flesh of the swine. And all that God said
"Thou Shalt Not do," they said "Thou Shalt Do." You
who read this book know the Christians are the great
false teachers of God, who care nothing for Allah's
(God's) law.

Since returning from prison, it has been hard for
me to adjust my eating habits. For many days in
prison, we had to eat two or three times a day in
order to make up for one meal a day through trying to
avoid eating the divinely-prohibited flesh of the
swine. This caused me and the others illness after we
had cleansed our stomachs of bad food and had begun
to eat at the proper time.

When we were eating the right food in the right way,
we had no doctor bills and no medical bills. There
were no medicines to be found in our medicine
cabinets. However, as soon as we changed and began
to eat between meals (24 hours), we began to call on
the doctor and his drugs — and it brought about one
complaint after another. I would never have suffered
today from bronchial asthma if I had not disobeyed
the law of the right foods to eat. Now I am on the way
back to try and adjust my life according to the way
Allah (God) taught me.

I experienced eating once a day for several years

and I experienced eating once every two days for a long time. Then I experienced eating one meal every three days (twice a week). I never had any symptoms of disease or sickness when I was eating once every 48 hours and once every three days. With this method, you feel as though you never were sick in all your life — even if you are a 100 years old.

Nothing shortens our lives but our foolish selves.

Proper Food for Body and Mind Equals Good Health

On the coming of God, according to the Bible and Holy Qur-an, He began to create a people that must and will enjoy a long life and good health. They will not suffer sickness or grief and sorrow. They will live lives of complete happiness.

The earth is full of food; but good health cannot enter our bodies until we have the proper food in the body and the proper food for thought. If we do not have the proper food for our way of thinking, we still cannot enjoy peace, good health, joy and gladness of heart.

We can eat the best food, we can take fasts for nine days or for 20 or 30 days if we want to; and we will still suffer if we do not feed the brain with the right food. These two bodies — the brain and digestive tract — have much in common with one another. Whatever hurts one hurts the other. We must treat both well.

The Bible teaches you that God gave the dead more life. He comes to give you more life and an abundance of life. How can He do that for us unless we help ourselves to the assistance He is helping us seek? We must help ourselves in this way to prolong our lives.

Obey and do all that Allah bids us. Think the way He thinks; the thoughts of good. Seek to be like Him, both physically and mentally. As the Holy Qur-an teaches us, when we have submitted ourselves entirely to the will of God, He then guides us into His path, His way of life. And then we come to enjoy the paradise of life in these words of the Holy Qur-an:

"O soul that is at rest,
Enter into My gardens,
Into My paradise among
Servants well pleased
And well pleasing."

This is what man has sought: the heaven within and the heaven without. If heaven does not begin within, we will never enjoy it on the outside. We do not go to a certain place for heaven. Nearly all of my followers and I are already in heaven (a peace of mind and contentment for the necessities of life, such as food, clothing, shelter, and without the enemy of fear and grief). And, with the protection of Almighty God, Allah, what more do we want?

If we went into another place, we still would not enjoy it more. Oh, certainly, we would be happy to live in a place where there was nothing but people like ourselves, thinking as we think and trying tto obey the law of God.

But still, within ourselves, we are happy because this evil world does not attract us anymore. We do not desire this kind of life that the wicked live. Our thoughts or minds feast upon the spirit of goodness.
Therefore, the spirit of evil cannot find a place among us to dwell.

Remember, life is what we make of it. Stay away from hog (the swine), the stinking tobacco weed, the hot fiery alcohol, wine, beer, drugs, foolishness, ignorance, madness, drunkenness, gambling, murdering, robbery, deceitfulness, lying, mockery and seeking to take advantage of your brother and your sister, and believe in the presence of God in the Person of Master Fard Muhammad, to Whom praises are due forever.

The Benefits of Eating Once A Day

As many people are writing to me for personal answers as to what we should and should not eat, I think it would lessen my work and be wise if you kept this book where you may refer to it when needed.

Many of my followers write and tell me of the results they are receiving from eating one meal a day or one meal every other day. This will produce good results and lengthen our lives. But children should not be forced to fast or to eat once a day or once every other day.

Children and babies should eat at least twice a day. If you are now eating three meals a day and you would like to eat one meal every other day, you should not — all of a sudden — change from three meals a day, every day, to one meal every other day.

First drop to two meals a day, then one meal a day, and then one meal every other day. It is better to do it this way so that you will not make yourself sick. And, if you eat every other day, do not begin your meal with heavy food.

I receive many questions in regard to meat, fish, and poultry. The main thing Allah, as well as the Holy Qur-an, reminds us of is that when it comes to meat and fish, Allah forbids us to eat the flesh of swine or of fish weighing 50 pounds or more.

Although some people will not eat fish at all, there are many fish that we can eat; some weighing as little as a pound or a pound and a half.

When eating fish, we should confine our fish-eating to those fish weighing between one and ten pounds. As I said previously do not eat the scavengers of the sea such as oysters, crabs, clams, snails, shrimp, eels, or catfish.

The catfish is a very filthy fish. He loves filth and is the pig of the water. Some people write in, complaining about the fish that swim on their sides, but these fish can be eaten.

Allah has taught me that chickens are not good for us to eat. They are quite filthy (inasmuch as they do not eat the cleanest of food), but we eat them.

We eat beef and lamb; but Allah also said that they are not very good for us. It is not a sin for us to eat them. It is not a sin for us to eat camels. But if we can find better food, we should not eat the above mentioned food. Many write and ask if they should eat meat at all. It is not a sin for you to eat meat, but it is a sin for you to eat the meat of the hog.

If we want to prolong our lives, it is best that we do not eat meat or do not eat it so often. Beef is very coarse and many of our people do not eat it because of that. Horsemeat can also be eaten. It is cleaner than the average meat. But we should not eat it unless we are extremely hungry and have nothing else to eat because it is a domestic animal and is gentle and close to the home.

It is not even a sin to eat rabbit. But since Allah said that the rabbit is so closely related to the house cat, we do not eat it. The rabbit, however, is cleaner than the house cat because he eats vegetables, roots and herbs and he does not eat insects or other animals.

Allah has said that no wild game should be eaten at all. Regardless of how you love deer meat, the deer is not good to eat. No game that run wild in the woods or birds that fly, with the exception of baby pigeons, called squabs, that have never flown away from the nest where they were born, should be eaten. Please do not eat coons, possums, turtles, turtle eggs, or frog legs. None of these are good for us.

A List of Foods
We Must Not Eat

Do not eat the swine flesh. It is forbidden by the divine law of Allah (God).

Do not eat field peas, black-eyed peas, speckled peas, red peas or brown peas.

Do not eat lima beans, or baby limas. Do not eat any bean but the small navy bean — the little brown pink ones, and the white ones.

Do not eat corn bread because it is very hard on the stomach, and not easily digested. Eat whole wheat bread, but not the whole grain. The whole grain is too hard to digest. Never eat freshly cooked bread. It rises and buckles in the stomach. Eating freshly cooked bread will shorten your life.

Do not eat the rich soy bean flour. Neither the flour nor the oil from the soy bean is good for our stomachs.

Do not eat the vegetable kale, nor sweet potatoes and white (Irish) potatoes, which are a staple food for people who live in frigid zones, or for people who cannot afford other vegetables.

The main thing you must do — I will repeat — is eat one meal a day, or once every 24 hours. And never eat — or even touch — the swine flesh.

When you begin eating once a day, certainly you will begin to lose weight until you are used to eating once a day. Then you will start gaining weight again. But fat is not wanted for health. It is an enemy to health.

You Don't Need Numerous Diets; Just Eat Once Daily

In the Christian world, you have innumerable food diets and numerous ways to prepare them — and these numbers are ever increasing.

We must remember that the Christian world commercializes on everything — even on the gospel of Jesus Christ (spiritual food).

God is visiting us to teach us — the Lost and Found members of God's family — to prolong our lives (give us more life and abundancy of life), as it is written.

By no means can we get this life from any other source. We must follow the guidance of Almighty God — Who appeared in the Person of Master Fard Muhammad, to Whom praise is due forever — and not the ways of the people whose diets have sent us calling the doctor and being hurried off to the hospital and from the hospital to our graves.

The white people called the Christian race, after they were driven out of the Holy Land and roamed the caves and hillsides of Europe, lived there for 2,000 years, eating raw food. They did not know how to cook anything, or the use of fire until Moses taught them.

Can we accept them and their way of life instead of Allah's? No, we will take Allah's will and His guidance. It goes something like this: Eat one meal a day. If this does not make you well, eat one meal every other day — nothing between meals.

And eat only the right foods. He said milk, bread and navy beans would lengthen our lives to 140 years. He did not give us a long list of different food diets and foods to confuse us on what to eat.

Cook your foods well done — especially animal

meat. Boiling your food until it is well done is better on your digestive system than baking and frying meats. Baking and frying it makes it about as hard on your digestive system as eating it raw. Never try to put a baked crust on any of your food except bread.

Drink plenty of wholesome milk. Eat butter, bread and fresh foods. If you eat fowl, lamb, squab and fish, cook it well done. Keep your food under steam — pressure cook it with the lid on.

Do not look up a variety of things to eat. Most vegetables are good to eat except those which you have been forbidden to eat, such as collard greens, black-eyed peas, and a lot of green cabbage sprouts.

Eat the white part of cabbage and cauliflower. Stay off those peanuts, coconuts, and nuts — period.

The Christian world eats according to taste. It eats — not for life, but for taste.

Cook well done whatever you eat. Cook bread throughly. If you have a refrigerator, put your leftover bread in it, or place it where it will keep moist and won't dry out. If that does not taste good, cook it over again. There is no such thing as stale bread. Let no bakery or anyone fool you. It is for your health.

If you do not have the knowledge of how to prepare your bread, seek a Muslim who knows how to prepare it. Some Muslim sister will teach you.

Give the corn bread back to the horses and the mules — that is their food. Do not eat grits or coarsely chopped corn. The corn is fit for you only in its milk stage.

Eat to live and not to die. Food, God said to me, keeps us here and takes us away. Three meals a day are needed by a savage beast but not by a human being. No human being should eat more than once a day.

Eat when you are hungry, if it is not until six or seven days. Let no one fool you about the above instructions. They will keep the doctor away from your bedroom and will prolong your life.

Keep from eating those sweets that are prepared to hurry you off to your grave. And you diabetics, eat only one meal a day. Stay away from that starchy food and sugar if you are a diabetic, and you won't have to get a doctor to pour insulin and other medicine into you to balance your life.

All that I have said in this book I have experienced myself.

Feeding Babies

Mothers should feed their babies from their breast milk if they possibly can, as this is the best.

When you are able to start feeding them on solid food, give them weak bean soup — not the highly seasoned, strong soup that you eat. You also can start them out with orange juice and mashed apples. This is done whenever you think the baby is able — after he is about three months old. This depends on the health of the baby and its age.

Plenty of good milk and good, thoroughly cooked bread are good for you and the baby.

We must not get the idea that we can nurse the baby with everything we eat. This is what will start sickness and disease in the family.

Some mothers are very careless. The baby can act as if he wants what mother is eating, and even if it is a beef steak, she will cut him a piece.

We create sickness right in our homes, from the cradle to the grave.

ORTHODOX JEWISH FOOD

A Muslim, according to the Holy Qur-an, should not fear to eat food that the Jews eat. And the Jews do not fear eating a Muslim's food, because they both eat the same type of foods.

Orthodox Muslims are very careful of what they eat. The only food we shun that they love are nuts. The Muslims are warned against eating nuts of any kind. And, they are warned against drinking the blood of the animals and fowls, because blood is the fluid of life.

Therefore, no human being should eat or drink the blood of anything. The Jews were warned against this by the teachings of Moses, the Servant of Allah.

Meat — Part 1

It is useless to keep repeating to you the same truth day and night, month after month, and year after year when you have it written in your book, the Bible. The main meat that our people like to eat is what they have been taught not to eat — the cheap and filthily-raised hog.

This is a divinely-prohibited flesh. This truth has been before our eyes ever since we have had permission from the white man to read the Bible. Nothing good is said about it in the Bible in Leviticus. The priests of Israel were warned not only against the eating of this prohibited, poisonous flesh, but that they should not even touch its carcass. But now the Christians, who claim they are better than all the religious people of the earth, not only touch the carcass, but eat the carcass — and then advise you and others to do the same.

Then, they say they are followers of Jesus, the son of God, while he himself was against the eating and the touching of this hog.

You can read a parable concerning this filthy swine: Jesus found a man possessed of evil spirits, and wanting to relieve the man of such evil spirits, he sent the evil spirits (devils) out of the man into the swine. The preachers (representatives of the son of God) and the priests know this to be true, but they preach that it is all right now to eat swine — and still say they are the beloved of Jesus. How could they be when they broke the laws of God by eating the swine? Nowhere in the scriptures does it bid us to break the law that God set up for this prohibited flesh.

The Christians laugh at my followers and me for not eating this filthy animal, as though they have an option from God and Jesus to eat it. It is the filthiest, ugliest and silliest animal, in whom nature did not put any shyness. Those who love to relish his flesh have very little shyness, as you can see today in the Christian Americans who love to go half nude and say that they are all right with God.

They say this with a stomach full of divinely-prohibited flesh, intoxicating drinks and now, on top of that, dope or drugs. Should America boast that she is a people following Christ or Jesus? Americans are making a mockery of God and His prophet Jesus. They hate His law of righteousness, health and decency.

The hog is a grafted animal, so says Allah to me—grafted from rat, cat and dog. Don't question me. This is what Allah has said, believe it, or let it alone.

You have witnessed that the rat is involved in the grafting of this hog in Isaiah 66:17. "They that sanctify themselves (self-claiming righteous of the Christians), and purify themselves in the gardens behind one tree in the midst, eating swine's flesh, and the abomination, and the mouse, shall be consumed together, saith the Lord."

He will kill them. He doesn't want them wilfully and knowingly eating such flesh, which is filled with poison in the shape of worms (trichina or pork worm) which gradually destroy humans as termites destroy timber. This filthy, evil worm can stand a temperature higher than any known flesh worm. He can't be seen with the naked eye. You have to get the microscope. Put a little piece of his flesh (fat part), or just grease a glass slide of the microscope with his flesh, take a look, and you will see him crawling around.

These worms begin in the stomach, weaving themselves to breed their families in the walls of the stomach; from there into the walls of the intestines; from there into our muscles, and from there into the spine and brains where no medicine can reach them and the victim dies with the disease that they produce with their presence.

White Christians represent pork as being good for you to eat. This is enough to teach you that they never wanted to obey the divine law, nor do they want black people to do so. It is one of the most commercialized meats in America, and wherever they can sell it.

Know The Truth about The Flesh of The Swine

In an earlier chapter of this book, I told you how Allah taught me about the birth of the swine, and that this animal was made only for the whites. Because theirs is a grafted race, they were made weaker physically through the man from whom they came (the black man). Since the body of the grafted is weaker than the original body, it would be easier for them to attract germs than the original man. You should not argue with me about this because all of the diseases that trouble us today — from social diseases to cancer — came from the white race, one way or the other.

Do not tell me about four or five hundred years or one thousand years; I am referring to this people's entire historical scope. They have had 6,000 years to mix with and poison our people. Some of you are foolish enough to accept all the blame. But God clears you of it. This refers to those who love the devils so much that they would like to dispute God about them. I am only teaching you the truth — take it or leave it.

They are too wise to dispute the truth. Read the story in the Bible in which Jesus met a man who was possessed of evil spirits. When the evil spirits recognized Jesus to be from God — knowing they would have no chance to contend with him over their presence in the man where they did not belong — they pleaded with Jesus to let them go into the swine, and Jesus agreed. The man who was possessed of evil spirits was none other than the American so-called Negro. The evil spirits in him are from the white race, who made him eat the divinely-prohibited flesh of the swine. The devils were allowed to go into the swine. They ran down a steep place into a lake or sea and perished.

Here the picture changes; the meaning changes a bit. The hog was made for the white race for medical purposes — not even for them to eat — but they could eat it if they wanted to, since they were created to be destroyed. They use this hog in much of their medical preparation, even in the German 606 (606 poisonous germs).

Allah taught me that one of these germs came from the swine. However, the white man will advise you to eat it. He would have you think the swine is cleaner now than he was in Jesus' time, but wouldn't God know — 4,000 years from Moses — if this swine would be clear of poison? You admit God is a Foreknower.

The whole story was twisted around. They want you to think God did not know about this process of the devils leaving the man and entering the swine until after it happened. Actually, God knew it was going to happen before it took place. Using deceit, they have succeeded in getting you to eat the swine as food, though it was made to produce a poisonous germ for medical purposes in curing the diseases of the white race.

This is how he makes you break all of the commandments of God. Because he is God's enemy and yours and mine, he has you break the divine law. We did this because we saw him doing it and at that time had no teacher of our own. These are the tricks of your hidden enemies and their own concocted religion called Christianity, which is deceiving and leading you to your doom with them.

I am your brother, and Allah has revealed to me the truth for your salvation. Jesus also prophesied that the truth would free you — that is, if you accept the truth. The thing you must understand in this parable of Jesus is that, actually, the visible swine could not have gone crazy and choked in the sea or lake, because the spirit of the devil was sent in them, The true meaning that you should understand is the swine that was choked to death in the sea after the spirit of the devil was taken out of the man represents the believers among the so-called American Negroes, and the swine that ran into the lake and perished represents the disbelievers among the so-called American Negroes who refuse to accept the truth. They are so obessed with the evil doings of the devils they will not accept their own salvation and will be choked into hell-fire with the devils.

As you have in the Bible, Lucifer's (Yakub') fall also represents the fall of his race. The lake or sea in which they choked and perished in the same lake mentioned in the Revelations of John — that all that had the mark of the beast, the representatives of the beast and the false prophets (priests and preachers of Christianity) referred to as being cast alive in a lake of fire.

I hope you understand. What I am trying to get over is that you who reject Allah and His true religion — entire submission to His will as the Arabs call it, Islam — will perish in the lake of fire with this race of

74

adversaries of Allah and His true religion, to which they refuse to submit. They now are trying to woo you into sharing hell-fire with them, though they know that you have a chance to go to heaven while they do not.

I cannot force you to halt your downhill plunge with them into the lake of fire. I have been missioned only to warn you in the simplest language. I cannot force you to go to hell or heaven.

Your sweethearting and wanting to marry them is like a frog trying to court a rattlesnake. The rattlesnake gives the frog freedom to do so because he intends to swallow the frog. Taking the death-dealing pill and the knife to destroy your future generations are examples. Socializing with them is no sign of justice, but a sign that they have deceived you into going to hell with them. Take it or leave it.

Live A Thousand Years

In the past, our appetite was our God. We ate as many times a day as we could find an appetite to. We worshipped our appetite as though it was our God. This shortens our lives.

Some of us have never gone a day without eating, unless we were sick and the doctor stopped us until his drugs could aid in killing the germ that eating three or four meals a day had caused.

We think we cannot miss a meal, unless we are unable to buy the next meal. So we wear out our stomachs that could possible live a thousand years, if cared for and protected from the enemies that will shorten and destroy our lives.

We can soon get accustomed to eating once a day and nothing between meals. After getting used to eating once a day, we can get used to eating once every two days. Our stomachs will not ask us for food — except at the time that we make a habit of putting food in them.

Surely one meal a day and eating the right kind of food at that meal will do away with much sickness and add many years to our lives. Try it for yourself.

Do not eat everything you see the Christians eat. That is why they have so many hospitals and must produce so many doctors every year.

Eat to live, and not to die, because how you eat does both — it keeps you here, and it takes you away. Do not fill up your stomach with sweets. Keep away from greasy foods.

Allah (God) has brought us this knowledge, in the Person of Master Fard Muhammad. Believe in Him,

obey and follow His teachings, and you will always be
happy.

Train Yourself to Eat As Allah Has Advised

To keep healthy and strong, and live a long time on this old earth, Allah said to me, in the Person of Master Fard Muhammad, eat one meal every two or three days. Do not be frightened, brothers and sisters, that with your meal hours being lengthened you may die or become too hungry.

You will live and you will not be hungry, after you have gotten your stomach used to the long intervals between meals. Your stomach will take food only when you give it food. And, it won't ask you for any food until that certain hour to which you have accustomed it to being fed.

I used to think like you, before the coming of our God and Saviour, in the Person of Master Fard Muhammad, To Whom Praise is due forever. I began practicing eating one meal every day — with no food in between. I got used to that within a couple of weeks. And, after a certain length of time, I tried eating once every two days, with nothing between but coffee.

I did not try to pour all of the cream and sugar out of the cream and sugar gowls into the coffee. I sweetened and creamed it as I had done when I was eating three meals a day, because we can live on cream and sugar for a long time. But it is not good that we do this through our coffee, for our health's sake. I felt better eating one meal every two days, or 48 hours, with nothing between.

I also tried eating one meal every 72 hours, as He had told me that if I ate one meal every three days I would never be sick, and I thought I would try it, before teaching it. So I did for a few months and I felt better than I felt when I was eating one meal every 48 hours. And, I can bear witness that I did not have the symptoms of illness at any time. My whole body felt light and my head was clear. I could almost hear insects crawling. (smile)

It is not so much what you eat when you begin eating one meal every day, or every two or three days, it is just that you do not eat foods that are against your health. I have described in this book, time and again, that which He pointed out to me. But most poor people like us eat the inexpensive food, because we do not have the money to buy expensive foods that rich millionaires eat. So, He prescribed for us dry navy beans and bread and milk.

There are some people asking about eating sardines. They are for us to eat only if we are traveling and cannot get other foods. But, please do not buy them, unless they are fresh when you can clean them, and not those that are packed already. There are some packed that are clean, but they are a little expensive. They are called Portuguese sardines.

There are other herbs that we can eat that are not mentioned here in this book. But please, whenever you decide on eating something that is not mentioned in this book, write me, because there are some on the market that are not good for you and me.

"The Death Way"

Under the system of this world, the baby is born wrestling with life and death, and death wins this struggle and throws the majority of us into our eternal graves before we reach the age of 50, and the remainder before we reach the short age of 100 years — when we should live 500 to 1,000 years. And the weakest one should live at least 100 years.

Why is our span of life so short? Because we try to follow and practice the way of the wicked, whose span of life was limited in the beginning of their time of 6,000 years. And, due to their lack of the essence of righteousness, and of eternal life, they care not for a long span of life.

‧They desire to shorten the span of life for the aboriginal people, who have no beginning or ending — and have done just that — because we have not lived the way of their life.

What we were and what we are given to eat and drink has shortened our life. The way we live — that short term of life from 12 to 30 years — is but a fleeting moment of the time we should live. The earth is an old, old earth, and the life that is in it is our life also. It produces us and it takes us back, as dead material to fertilize the life germ that is yet to be made into man.

We should live far longer than we have — as long as we see where we came from, and that the material that made up our bodies is still alive. But, what has happened to us? We were fed with death at the very beginning — the wrong food and drink, given to us when we were babies by our wicked enemies, until today, we think that it is a mistake to contemplate living 100 or more years; not to think of 1,000 year. We think that is impossible.

But it is no more impossible for us today to live 800 or 900 years, than it was for Methuselah, who lived 969 years (each year carrying 12 months like the ones we have today).

The Holy Qur-an teaches us that a year with Allah has always been 12 months. And the civilizations of earth must count their years according to the time it takes the earth to rotate around the sun, and get itself into position. That, the astronomers teach us, will give us a more correct way of counting the time.

We and our sons and daughters are fed on poisonous foods, milk and water, from the start of life. This way of eating like the beasts soon robs us of life, and we go away within a few years.

The baby eats poisonous animals, fowls and vegetables and drinks milk that is not his milk — it belongs to the cow's baby, goat's baby and horse's baby. Here the child is reared on animals' and cattle's food.

This is why we have such a great percentage of delinquency among minors. The child is not fed from his mother's breast — she is too proud of her form. Therefore, she lets the cow and other animals nurse her new-born baby. And, the baby cannot have too much love for its mother. It loves the bottle that its food is in — food that his mother robbed from the cow's baby to feed her own baby.

When the baby reaches the age of 10, and if it is a male, most of them begin to indulge in drinking alcoholic beverages and using tobacco in one form or another.

Alcohol and tobacco, with their poisonous effect upon the male, cut his life down, as far as his reproductive organs are concerned. He is unable to produce his own kind. And, nowadays, with dope added to all of the above-mentioned poisonous food and drinks, we can easily say with truth, that the people are committing suicide.

In a few days (years), they lose sexual desires. Tobacco and whiskey will most certainly destroy it. The flesh of swine and alcoholic drinks will give a false impression of feeling to the victim — that you are strong and able to finish the course — but you can't depend on it. Soon, one finds himself needing strength again and again — not to think of how venereal diseases destroy those who indulge in the extremes of life.

Let us eat to live, as Allah (God) has taught me.

Do Not Take Birth Control Pills

It is Allah's (God's) love and my love, as His Messenger, to teach you and keep you aware of the tricks the devil devises to trap you into accepting death and not life. As it is written, Allah (God) has come to you to save you from death and destruction by the wicked and to register you in the book of the living (the Black Nation) with unlimited future.

He has declared that we are the true members of the Nation of Islam, the righteous, who shall never be removed from the earth by any foe. He even laughs at plans to destroy the nation of righteous.

The birth control law the enemy is preparing for you, with the aid of their angels, the blind, deaf and dumb black preachers and ignorant black politicians, is not concerned about your future. The white priest knows what these plans will do for you. They know that Christianity has been exposed to the civilized world as nothing less than bait to enslave the black people of earth, the original people who serve the white race as slaves. He offers you death in a pill for your future generations of children.

He tells you what it is going to do to you. But it is like telling a would-be suicide: "Here is the loaded gun. Put it to your silly head, and blow your brains out." Then he stands aside, throws up his arms and says to the world that he is not responsible for your suicide. This is what you do when you swallow the pills. He knows you are blind, deaf, and dumb.

I know you do not know the plans and secrets of your enemies, but Allah and His Messenger have known for a long time — for this was ascertained when we first learned to read the history of Pharaoh, who sought to destroy the future of Israel through the midwives. We know that this, too, is aimed at you in these last days.

We know by the words of the Holy Qur-an on this attempt to destroy your newborn babies; to destroy the very seed of you. You also are warned against birth control law. They say you are not able to provide for the many children with which Allah (God) is blessing you. They say you should be willing to stop giving birth to children they will have to feed.

Who is responsible? Is it not the slave master's and his children's fault that you are not able to care for your family? It is theirs not yours. Why don't they divide the country with you, give you a few of these United States and let you raise all the children you want so you can provide a proper living for them.

But, no! He would rather you were dead than to see you living free of his authority and power to enslave and murder you at will.

You are aware of this, but yet you are a fool. You do not understand that they are after your life — and you are seeking death by following and agreeing with them to destroy you and your Nation.

The earth belongs to the black nation, and its people will rule it in the near future. God never gave the whites any of the earth. He only gave them time to live on it; time to make fools of you and me. However, that time was limited, and I now can say in truth, that "time is up."

I will defend the interest and life of my people, even at the destruction of my own life, and the lives of those who follow me — for that is why I have been raised among you. It is a disgrace upon us black people of America to permit ourselves and our future generations to be cut off and destroyed by ignorant, foolish, pleasure-seeking girls and women of our own, who do not know what they are doing when they swallow the birth control pill.

I repeat: If you accept Allah (God) and follow me and if you give birth to 100 children, each of you girls and women is considered more blessed and right in the eyes of Allah (God) than those who try to kill the birth seed.

Because of the advice of those who hate you and hope that you destroy yourselves, the clergy — the priests and elders — is united to help deceive you. The Catholic religion is our greatest enemy today. It seeks to woo you into its net where your future will be hopeless in the Hereafter. This old scheme of attempting to destroy the so-called Negro when the day of his salvation comes to him from God, has long been known by us and Allah (God). The nation of righteous is fully prepared to meet it.

Jehovah thwarted Pharoah's wicked plan to prosper through destroying the future of Israel. Pharaoh was afraid of Israel's population, who was populating Egypt faster than the Egyptians. However, he did not want the Israelites to leave Israel. He decided to kill off the male children, which would have stopped Israel from increasing her nation. The birth control laws employed by the white race were used by his father, Yacub. It is no new thing today. He does not teach you this, nor does he teach you the sciences of modern warfare or chemistry. Of course, we do not care to learn any more about warfare, for it is the purpose of God to erase war from the human family. He now plans to destroy those who delight in making war against humanity.

Who said the white man had to carry us forever? Who gave him the right to cut our birth rate so that he could take care of a small number of us? Who is willing to swallow the pill? The 22,000,000 so-called Negroes can be placed in Africa or Asia. The country is so large, they would not know they were there. Or they could be put on an island in the Pacific. But he want to exterminate all of them with the pills so that he and his people can have free reign of the earth. But he should have reckoned with Allah (God), Who has come for the purpose of saving the poor, black man from their wicked plans.

The Negro has been a group of people, held in the hands of the white man, for 400 years and yet, today, he is like a lazy horse or dog who does not want to leave his master because of fear — and has taken all kinds of abuse in order to get a little food or whatever the master has to give. It is a shame. It is not because of lack of education, but because he holds the offer of Allah (God) in mockery.

But this pill is a bold offer of death, openly made, inviting the Indians and so-called Negroes to accept death — and also the people they have under their power in the Pacific islands. It is accepting extermination through a harmless looking pill, designed to take away the future birth of our Nation. Think well, you "white Christian lovers." You sign up to be swallowed up.

Israel was taken into a country where she could do all of the populating she wanted to without the interference of Pharaoh. Allah (God) had Pharaoh drown in the Red Sea, and the white race is going to be thrown into a lake of fire for its plans against the so-called Negro.

I shall always rise to your defense against such an artful, wicked race of people, who has nothing in mind but death for the black man — its scheme covered with a semi-bait of good. Once you have swallowed the birth control pill, it is death.

Food And Health

I have said to eat no peas. At that time, I did not think about what we call sweet peas, which grow into pods. They can be eaten, but not field peas. I had reference to field peas, such as black-eyed peas, brown, yellow, and black peas (there are some black field peas).

We all know that food and health keep us here and the same makes us sick and takes us away — if we do not make a practice of eating the right food and drinks that will not make us sick and cause an early death.

The way that Almighty God Allah, in the Person of Master Fard Muhammad, to Whom praise is due forever, has taught us, makes sense.

When we get used to eating one meal a day, or every 24 hours, we start eating once every two days, which will give to you and me better results than eating one meal a day. Even eating one meal a day — and eating the right kind of food and having a pure drink — will bring us health and prolonged life of which we would not even dream. You will not be sick if you eat correctly. And let what you drink be pure — that which will not harm the body.

Again, you wiill agree with me that we Americans are a very gluttonous people and that we prepare our own sick bed, hospital bills, and undertaker bills with what we eat and what we drink. And besides this comes a sick mind, and after a sick mind comes death.

You just try eating and drinking and living at peace with yourself and others, and you will write me and tell me that these words are true.

As for the swine (hog), he is well known to be an animal that we should not take for food, because he puts an almost incurable disease in those who eat his flesh.

Foods to Avoid

We should not be asking questions about what kind of foods to eat as much as we should be trying to eat one meal a day. This is where good health and the prolongation of life come from. Good health and the prolongation of life come from abstaining from filling our stomachs too frequently with food of any kind — good or bad. Of this I can assure you from self-experience.

If we keep food going into our stomachs only once every 24 hours or 48 hours, and do not get the foolish idea that this cannot be done, then we can train our stomachs to eat once a week and our stomachs will not call for food more than once a week. This has been tried. If we could eat one meal a week, we could live as long as Methuselah.

We can get away from eating animal flesh and all kinds of scavanger sea foods. Do not eat large fish that weigh over 50 pounds — such as canned tuna. Sometimes this canned tuna comes from a fish that weighs nearly a thousand pounds or more. Do not eat halibut, catfish, or carp.

There is a cheap fish called buffalo (white buffalo) that you can eat. But do not eat any stale fish if you can help it.

Even fish is not very good for us, due to their animal-like instincts in the water. But we eat them, and it is not a sin to eat them (edible fish).

Many of the bass fish that are found in lakes, rivers, and running stream water are good to eat. White fish, channel trout (which is better), river trout and most perch are good to eat. You may eat fish that weigh from one and a half to four or five pounds.

We were reared on the animal flesh that was the divinely-prohibited flesh (the hog). We must not eat or put our hands on the carcass of the hog, or sit around a place where it is being slaughtered or cooked. We should not even get the odor of it in our nostrils. It is a sin to deliberately stand and smell it being slaughtered or cooked. The devil did this harm to you and me and to the people all over the earth. Of course, we cannot blame him for doing this, because he was not created to do righteousness, anyway. Do not think hard of them for anything they do or teach you to do, because they are just doing their job. Nature has made them to be as they are. I pray Allah that He will remove them from the planet earth, so they will not deceive and misguide people from the right way.

Eat only one meal a day and do not take food between meals, unless you are sick. A person that is sick and weak is excluded from the above said time of eating.

Remember, do not eat those ugly horse beans that you have been eating (lima beans, field peas, etc.). Eat only small navy beans. They are white and pink in color. There are also large beans of the same color, but do not eat the great big beans — eat the small ones. Cook them thoroughly. Feed them to your children.

Do not eat freshly baked cakes. Give them a day to dry out, after baking. Do not ever hurry bread to bake, because it is better for us if it has been baked twice.

Stay away from eating fried foods. Do not make a habit of filling your stomach with aged cheese. Eat cream cheese as much as possible, as it is better for your digestive system.

Stay away from eating all meats and vegetables that are canned in metal cans as much as possible. Sometimes we are force to eat them because we do not have any other. Try and get your food canned in jars; or while the food is in season, buy it and can it in glass jars yourself. If you eat a vegetable meal, try to get fresh vegetables, if you can purchase them from a market.

Remember to eat one meal a day, regardless to your type of work. You can live on one meal a day. This will help keep your doctor away from your door. Of course, eating one meal every two days or three days is even better, but you are not going to apply yourself to eating once every two or three days, so try and eat only one meal every 24 hours. Make a habit of this and you will feel better and have fewer ailments.

The Safest Way to Eat

The safest way of all to eat is to stop eating so often (three meals a day and meals between those three meals). In the past, our appetites were as the appetites of swine. The swine has no certain time to eat. It will eat until it is sick and has to lie down, but as soon as it finds a vacancy in its stomach, it eats more food. It doesn't matter what kind of food it may be; the swine eats anything. The swine's life is very short, because it comes here eating itself to death, and death soon takes it away.

We eat too much and too often, and we eat the wrong food (poisonous foods). Most of our drinks are poisonous.

Allah has blesed America with the best of foods and with good water that is plentiful. America has been blessed with everything that she could desire, but after all of these blessings, she is ungrateful and turns good things into bad, and wages a war against the God of good and His people.

After telling the slaves they were free, America kept them here in order to prey upon them. Now today, many of the slaves wish to be free of America, but her reply by her actions to our wanting to be free is "no." And America continues to give the so-called Negroes the same bad food and drink that her (America's) fathers did in the days of slavery.

America's markets are loaded with swine, and loaded with vegetables and fruits which are preserved and made to look beautiful by having poisonous chemicals poured upon them. There are thousands, and hundreds of thousands of herds of cattle and sheep and there are hundreds of thousands of fowls. Yet, Americans decorate their tables with the divinely-prohibited flesh — the swine — and represent themselves as being the true Christian followers of Jesus.

Americans have poisonous whiskey and wine by the barrels and vats all over the country, yet when this does not make them intoxicated (drunk) and crazy enough, they resort to drugs (the poisonous weeds).

Allah has blessed them with so much bread that they set whole fields of good wheat on fire. They burn up the wheat in order to obtain higher prices for it. They are crazy over money and wealth.

Now today, Allah threatens America with all kinds of plagues — not one kind, but many kinds. Allah withholds the rains from her wheatfields; sends terrific cold and snow upon her fertile bread basket areas; kills her cattle, livestock and fowls; and kills her fish that are inland in ponds and rivers, with droughts.

All of these plagues are falling upon America because she is against God's giving freedom, justice, and equality to the so-called Negroes, whose labor she has had for 400 years. Because of America's having broken the Divine Law which prohibits eating swine flesh, and because of her having fed this forbidden meat to her slaves and to other nations of the earth, Allah (God) is now taking His blessings away from her.

The Poisonous Animal Eater

God, in the Bible, through his prophets, has condemned the eating of the poisonous animal (swine).

Leviticus 11:7-8 "And the swine, though he divide the hoof, and be cloven-footed, yet he cheweth not the cud; he is unclean to you. Of their flesh shall ye not eat, and their carcass shall ye not touch; they are unclean to you."

The dietary law given to Israel by Moses is true today. Israel was given the proper food to eat Jehovah approved for them, and that which was forbidden to eat we should not eat today.

The Christians have said that since Jesus the swine is good to eat, because Jesus made it good in his teachings. But this is all false and a shield for the Christians' eating the divinely-prohibited flesh of the filthy swine. They even teach you that he has a poison in his flesh. They call it the trichina worm, that is only revealed under a microscope. High school children have microscope sets to see this worm in the flesh of swine. But yet they eat it. Why? Because their teacher eats it and their teacher was the slave master and his children. The white race teaches that we should obey the law of God, but they themselves disobey. And they want you to disobey the law of God. Why? Because they are the devil-opponents of righteousness and all the right laws given from the author of righteousness. They want you and me to disobey Allah's laws, so that we will come under the curse and destruction of Almighty God, Allah, as they know they are doomed and they hope that you and I will suffer the same.

95

Through the eye of the microscope, we see this poisonous worm, that will creep in our own flesh if we eat the poisonous animal, swine, hog, or whatever you may call him.

The nature of the hog is to eat and thrive on anything edible — filth, or clean food. But, clean food will not remove the pork worm (trichina). The worm travels from our mouth into our stomach; from our stomach into the walls of the intestines; from the walls of the intestines, he weaves his way into the muscles of our body; from there, into the spinal cord and up to our soft gray matter (brain). He is there to stay, until the preacher says "from dust we came, and to dust we returneth."

The hog or swine causes many ailments of various symptoms (names) mentioned. Medical scientists know what has caused these symptoms that we are troubled with . The medical scientists know that the hog is unfit for our consumption. Medical scientists also know that the swine will shorten our lives. But, medical scientists also know that they can get rich from the effect of the swine in our bodies, as the hog raiser can get rich by selling 100 or 200 pounds of poison that will take us away gradually. It does not take us away quickly, but gradually. The pork worm will finally bring you and me to our grave.

Not to think of eating the swine, Leviticus mentions in the 8th verse that we shall not even touch the carcass of the swine. But, we are not only touching the carcass, we are eating the carcass.

Isaiah 66:17 condemns the people who think it is all right to eat the swine, just because white people eat it, and they think they can be holy in the presence of God, or in a religion they call Christianity (which they received and have been taught is a God-verified religion). This is wrong. God never verified Christianity as being His religion. If He did, He changed His Mind when he taught the prophets to submit to Him. His religion is entire submission to Him. The Arabic work for this is Islam, which means to submit.

There are so many little new groups that call themselves sanctified, holy, Jesusified, Christified, and Godified. Such people should read this chapter, Isaiah 66:17-18.

"They that sanctify themselves, and purify themselves in the gardens behind one in the midst (the one in the midst is the preacher, inviting them to disobey the law of God), eating swine's flesh, and the abomination, and the mouse, shall be consumed together, saith the Lord."

Death is for you who eat the swine. God will not accept swine eaters as His people, after knowledge that the swine is a divinely-prohibited flesh. The hog (swine), God has taught me, in the Person of Master Fard Muhammad, To Whom praise is due forever, was made from the grafting of cat and dog. The rat is mentioned in the above quoted verse of Isaiah, but the cat and dog are not mentioned. The white theologians knew that if they had given the names of these two animals (the cat and the dog), you would have probably not accepted the hog. But, Who is better knowing than Allah.

The hog was made, Allah taught me, for medical purposes, to cure the white man's many diseases, since he had been grafted out of the black man, and he attracted germs and diseases easily that were possibly incurable. At that time, the Arab medical scientists did not have anything that would kill most, or probably all, of his diseases, so they made a medicine for him — that is the hog. The hog contains, Allah said to me, 999 poisonous germs. This is what makes up the hog. And, the Christian will look at you, with a Bible at home and in his pocket, and say, if you do not eat it, "what is wrong with the hog?" They will even ask you what is wrong with strong alcoholic drinks (whiskey, beer, and wine). This proves beyond a shadow of a doubt that we have been reared and taught by an enemy of God, the real devil in person (the white race). Therefore, we are before God, today, with the sin of the white man, which He offers to forgive us for, if we now will accept the truth and will walk and practice righteousness, in the path of the righteous.

In the 17th verse the swine is called the abomination (this means hated). It is true that all good Muslims hate a swine. Some places, in the dominant areas of Islam, you will be killed if you carry any swine among them.

See Isaiah 66:18: "For I know their works and their thoughts: it shall come, that I will gather all nations and tongues; and they shall come, and see my glory."

The glory means the right way that He will teach the people in the last days; that He will approve of our doing what He gives to us in the Resurrection. He knows your works that ignore His law of righteousness, given to His prophets of old, and your self-centered thoughts, or your thinking that you can deceive others, while breaking the law of God, into thinking you are right in eating the swine. But, He has promised death to you in the 17th verse. He will consume such people all together.

We must remember that these warnings given in the 17th and 18th verses of Isaiah are referring to the general resurrection, and the accountability of our actions and disobedience to the law of God, because the 18th verse says, "... it shall come that I will gather all nations and tongues."

This is also prophesied in Matthew 25:32: "And before him shall be gathered all nations..."

Since the white race is more guilty than anyone else of breaking the law of Allah (God), He threatens with chastisement and total destruction. We may quote Isaiah 65:15. It reads like this: "And ye shall leave your name for a curse unto my chosen: for the Lord God shall slay thee (the disobedient white race), and call his servants by another name."

Here, we are warned that God will not accept us in the name of the white race, because He has another name that He will call us by, and He mentions this throughout Isaiah and the New Testament. We must have a name of God and not the name of an enemy of God.

Isaiah 56:1-5: "I am sought of them that asked not for (The lost-found members of the Black Nation are the ones who never sought after Allah, because they did not know how. The enemy did not teach them how to seek Allah, since they did not obey Allah, themselves); I am found to them (lost-found Black people — so-called Negro) that sought me not: I said, Behold me, behold me, unto a nation that was not called by my name.

"I have spread out my hands all the day unto a rebellious people, which walketh in a way that was not good (This is referring to Israel, to whom God sent prophet after prophet, to guide them into the right way, who rebelled against right guidance and then made a religion called Christianity, after their way of thinking, and put the name of Jesus on that religion to make us drink down the falsity they added to Jesus' teachings), after their own thoughts; A people that provoketh me to anger continually to my face; that sacrificeth in gardens, and burneth incense upon altars of brick (they barbecue the hog upon bricks and call it their barbecue stand); which remain among the graves (the graves mean their homes),...which eat swine's flesh, and broth of the abominable things is in their vessels (this is referring to hog or swine in their vessels); which say, stand by thyself (This is referring to the Muslims, when it says stand by thyself), come not mean only Israel or the white race, but the white race has made the so-called Negro follow his religion, say the same and especially those who claim santification in Christianity.)

"These are a smoke (the offensive smell of the cooking of swine flesh)...a fire that burneth all the day (the Christian is cooking the flesh of the swine all day long and the Muslims and the obedient servant of Allah (God), smell this flesh, prohibited by God, which is a stink to their nostrils, being cooked. They feel they are guilty of being partakers of the cooking and eating of the swine flesh, by smelling the poisonous odor.)''

Keep away from the filthy swine. Do as Allah (God) bids you. Do not eat its flesh or touch its carcass.

Beautiful Appearance and Long Life

Allah, in the person of Master Fard Muhammad, to Whom praise is due forever, came to give us a spiritual life which would automatically give us a physical life of Himself (the life of the righteous), which we lost by following other than righteous guides.

We cannot be successful in making the progress of a spiritual life, unless we have the guidance for the physical life. This guidance comes to us through laws, rules and regulations of our physical life.

We must make this teaching of eating once a day binding upon us, as a law, in order to get any good from it, as Allah (God) desires. The purpose of these dietary laws and the time that we should partake of food is to lengthen our lives, by ridding us of the greedy desire to eat three times a day and between meals if we are offered food.

The main purpose of this teaching, "How to Eat to Live," is to prolong our lives.

Beauty appearance is destroyed in us — not just our facial appearance, but the most beautiful appearance about us, our characteristics (the way we act and practice our way of life). We achieve one of the greatest beauties when we achieve the spiritual beauty and characteristics through practicing them. We achieve the spiritual beauty through practicing or carrying into practice the spiritual laws.

We know that we have been made ugly by our enemies' rearing of our parents. We know that many of our people throughout the earth have been made ugly by not practicing culture that would beautify them. But we are blessed that God, Himself, has visited us to guide us in His way. What people on the earth has God visited in person today, other than you and me here in America?

The Wisdom that He teaches us is the Wisdom of God and of the Gods. It is Supreme Wisdom, because it is above and far ahead of what we have ever heard and what we see practiced by others today. Should we not obey that which is good for us, when we are members of the nation of good? Why should we not practice that which is good for us?

It has come to us and Allah (God) has said that it is ourselves that He is giving to us. Should we not accept the good for ourselves, instead of accepting evil and disobedience to the law of goodness, when the Bible verifies this truth?

Why should you and I not accept such good teaching and practice it? It will do away with sickness and keep death standing outside our doors for a long time — for many years. Think over Methuselah and Noah who kept death standing outside of the door for nearly one thousand years. Now we cannot stay here one century, which in one tenth of that time. We invite death inside the door, instead of obeying a law of God that will keep it outside for a long time.

Eat one meal a day. Stay away from the hog, of which 10 ounces takes away from you, God has said, three one-hundredths per cent of the beauty appearance.

This civilization has a thousand and one things for

you to eat. It is not necessary for you to go around trying to eat everything people say to eat to have good health. But, what you eat, let it be good and do not eat yourself to death at that one meal a day. This book has described to you good, common food. You do not have to be rich to purchase it.

And I would not like you to follow the Bible in Genesis, where Adam is told to go and eat of all the herbs of the earth. There are some poisonous herbs that would have killed Adam. This is a mistake that the theologians put in the Bible. You cannot eat all herbs; some of them will kill you. But, eat the best of herbs that God approves for you and me and do not think He approved of Adam' eating all the herbs of the earth.

Divinely Prohibited Flesh

Good health can be enjoyed by obeying the teachings of God (who came in the Person of Master Fard Muhammad. To Whom Praise is due forever), that is, by eating one meal every 24 hours (one meal a day).

It is not so much eating various kinds of food as it is not eating food of any kind too often. Of course, we know the Divinely prohibited flesh of the swine is totally forbidden not only to eat, but we are even forbidden to touch or handle the swine. It is punishable under the law of God to eat the swine.

Many of the readers may think that it is all right with God for them to do as they please about His laws, but we are punished for willfully disobeying the laws of God, regardless to how small or how great the offense may be.

The Christians have been eating the swine for four thousand years. Now, their punishment is total destruction by fire.

The white race was not made to obey the Divine Law. They were made to oppose it, therefore following after them and doing what they do will lead you to hell. It is no excuse for you. The average so-called Negro thinks it is all right for him to be evil too, but we are two different peoples. The so-called American Negro is a Divine member lost from the Divine circle, while the slave master, who has been his teacher, is an enemy to God, by nature. This is why the Bible teaches you that hell was created for them the day they were made.

So, do not practice the evil things that the white

race is doing, as you are following them now, If they pull off their clothes, you will pull off yours. Do you think you have an option to ignore divine law, while you do not? A doom is set for the whole race of them, and you will share their doom with them if you continue to eat and drink intoxicating drinks just because you see them doing such things and going nude in public (women with dresses above their knees and men wearing just trunks in public). You are following one of the most filthy things that even an animal could follow, by doing such things. White people do this to tempt you to do the same so that you can share hell fire with them.

Eat one meal a day and eat good food as has been prescribed for you in this book.

Poisonous Food and Water

If what we eat and drink keeps us alive, then we must be careful of what we eat and drink, because the same that keeps us alive can bring death to our life, as there are so many of us who do not know the kind of food and drink that we should eat and drink for long life.

Living under the guidance of the enemy of right and the God of the unrighteous is a very dangerous position to be in. This is just the position you and I, the poor, righteous so-called Negroes (lost-found members of the aboriginal Black Nation), are living in. Poisonous food and water we are now eating and drinking — sometimes too much poison to kill poison that is in our food and drinks. And, maybe it is the wrong poison for us human beings, whether it is in food or in drinks.

Take, for instance, the use of flouride, chloride, and sodium, which if not used correctly can destroy our entire life. Maybe it is best to find something else that will clear our water without killing both us and the poison in our food and water.

The scientist should not advocate the use of such poisonous chemicals as flouride, chloride, and sodium, which may have a bad effect on our brains and our human reproductive organs. The scientist that uses such poison on human beings wants to either minimize the birth rates or cause the extinction of a people.

D.D.T., which is sprayed on food while it is growing up from the earth, is also a poison that should not be put into the human body, regardless of the desire to kill the insects, that loves to dine on the same food on which we dine. The poison may not take instant affect on us, as it does the insects, but it can, over the long years, help shorten the span of our lives. We live in a world commercializing on everything where money is involved, and this has speeded production of everything but human lives, in order to fill the demand of the people. This has caused many scientists to overlook the dangerous effects that such fast production has on the health of the people. Therefore, the only way out for us, the poor Lost-Found, is to seek refuge and guidance in Allah for our protection from evil plannings and doings of Satan.

Allah (God) has pointed out to us in both the Bible and the Holy Qur-an that right foods for us to eat and He has pointed out the poisonous food and drinks. Follow His guidance or suffer the consequences.

Do not eat the swine — do not even touch it. Just stop eating the swine flesh and your life will be expanded. Stay off that grandmother's old fashioned corn bread and black-eyed peas, and those quick 15 minute biscuits made with baking powder. Put yeast in your bread and let it sour and rise and then bake it. Eat and drink to live, not to die.

Bad Food Causes Us to Look Old

The number one thing you should not eat is the hog (swine). You should also not eat field peas, lima beans, soy beans, bad stale beef (rotten beef), frozen stale turkey and chicken (Some of the turkey has been in cold storage so long that when it is thawed, it begins to disintegrate).

Try eating fresh food and do not eat stale, rotten food that will destroy your health — keeping the doctor around your home trying to administer drugs for the poison you have eaten, which you could have avoided — and take you to your grave very quickly.

There is also bad, stale fish for sale — all but rotten — that some of you buy and eat. Do not eat such rotten food, if you want to live long. If you want to live a short life, that is up to you. Eating bad food will soon shorten your life.

Do not eat canned meats, if you can help it, or canned beans, if you can buy fresh ones. Do not eat any canned goods, if you can find fresh food. Most of us can purchase fresh food from the market.

Some of you buy meats from the Jewish stores and some of you believe that all the Jewish people are religious Orthodox Jews and will not eat or sell bad meats, but you are wrong. There are "Christian" Jews who will eat everything and drink almost everything. The merchandise of these Jews must be shunned, if you desire to live.

We use the name Orthodox to refer to religious Jews who want to follow the law of Moses, their prophet, and who want to eat the food that he prescribed for them.

The Holy Qur-an teaches us that their food (meaning the food of the religious Jews) is good for us and our food is good for them. That is true, so long as both of us are eating the food that Allah prescribes.

Do not hasten the cooking of your food — not even your bread. Bread should be baked slowly, so that it will bake thoroughly. Do not eat freshly baked bread; let it be at least a day or two old. There is no such thing as stale bread. When the bread is a day or two old, it is better for our stomachs.

Eat the kind of vegetables that are prescribed for you in this book and do not eat nuts of any kind. They are not good for us. They are too hard on our digestive systems.

Bad food causes us to look old. The skin of those who eat such bad foods is tight and drawn. All the foods mentioned above are bad for our appearance.

The Pig

The hog takes away the beautiful appearance of people and takes away their shyness. The people who eat the hog have no shyness because they eat the hog. Nature did not give the hog any shyness. God, in the Person of Master Fard Muhammad, taught me that the scientists have found that the hog carries 999 poisonous germs in it and they are not 100 per cent poison, but nearly 1000 per cent poison. The swine takes away our life gradually and creates worms in our bodies.

110

The worms eat away our digestive tracts and cause bad thinking, because once they get into the spinal cord, they make their way to the brain and there they begin to affect the way of thinking, until they have eaten your life away. They are parasitic worms, referred to as pork or trichina worms. They cannot be seen by the naked eye — only under a microscope. They destroy three one-hundredths per cent of the beauty appearance of the eater, besides giving him fever, chills and headaches. Hayfever is also common among swine eaters.

The Poisonous Drinks

To drink whiskey, beer and wine when they have a high alcoholic content is against your and my health. These drinks have a tendency to be habit forming. When we become habitual drinkers, we are destroying our lives. If you want to live, you should not drink such beverages. You should not even drink a lot of soda pop. Some intelligent people will not drink one bottle of soda pop.

There are many bad drinks. Some water is poisonous for us to drink. There is water even in Chicago that is not good for our health. It is not pure enough. Water should be at least 99 per cent pure in order for it to be good for humans to drink.

Tobacco

If you want to live, stop smoking and chewing the poisonous weed (tobacco). Some of us are foolish enough to refer to our parents who chewed it and were

75 or 80 years old. That does not mean it was not harming them. Any medical scientist will tell you that the tobacco weed is a very poisonous weed.

The poison it contains is called nicotine. The full extent of the poisonous nicotine has not yet been known to scientists. Nicotine produces a tar-like substance wherever it is used — on the lips, fingers and in the mouth all the way down to the lungs.

Manufacturers are trying to put something like a filter on cigarettes that will keep the nicotine from going into your mouth, but this will not prevent you from getting some of it into your body. Tobacco is a weed that should not be used.

The poison which tobacco contains is what pacifies the smoker, who thinks he is feeling fine. Due to your habit of using the tobacco, you think it is giving you a sort of pacification, just like other drugs which make a patient feel that his nerves are better from the use of them.

Since Allah revealed this to us, the medical scientists and the government of America now acknowledge and admit some of the harm tobacco causes (You will find that the scientists and the government will admit most of the truth that Allah has revealed to us). They warn the users of tobacco that it is poisonous and that it creates lung cancer in tobacco users.

Tobacco and alcoholic beverages also affect the organs of reproduction of young men. You should never use tobacco, whiskey, beer or wine. They ruin the reproductive organs and waste away the man power. Tobacco and alcoholic beverages also have this destructive effect upon the reproductive organs of women.

Little Pure Food on Market:

There is no way we can ever enjoy good health unless we obey the teacher of health, Who advises us the proper way to eat. No people has ever been as fortunate as the Lost and Found members of the Black Nation (so-called Negroes), to receive guidance of life from God, Himself, present among them — the God who will bring about a total change of civilizations of this world; Who has the histories of how people practice a way of life for themselves back into the hundreds of thousands, millions and billions of years. Should He not know the best way to eat to live?

The Devil is a race of people for experimental purposes, whose way of life the people of the God of truth, justice and righteousness did not intend to follow, but have followed for a short time.

Remember our success is obedience to the Will of the God of truth, justice and righteousness, as we have been obedient to the devil in following and practicing other than truth, justice and righteousness. What we eat, I will repeat, keeps us here and takes us away. This is God's teaching to me, and it is so logical that there are no questions.

This race of people experiments on everything other than good. This includes what they grow and prepare for us to eat. There is very little pure food on the market today. And, there will not be any pure food on the market tomorrow, if they prepare it for you, because they are experimenting on your life to see what can take you away and what they can keep you here with for a certain length of time. Our lives are limited by what we eat that this race of people (meaning white devils) prepares for us.

The earth brings forth good food the natural way, but the food is poisoned by other ways. The fertilization process they use and the preservatives are all poisonous. They know in their limited time of six thousand years to rule that they are experimenting on themselves and us, too. Even the very earth is poisoned where they are experimenting on growing food for their markets, because it is the almighty dollar they seek and not the almighty health and long life for you and me.

Good will help the enemy devil, but since by nature they are not made of good, they cannot prosper under that which they do not practice.

Eat one meal a day and get the best you can out of what is before you.

The most important thing of health which prolongs life is accomplished by not eating poison food, which shortens our lives and brings disease into the body. This is accomplished, secondly, by not feeding the stomach too often.

All the white race, referred to as the Christian European race, eats too often. From two to four or five times a day, they are feeding their stomachs with some type of food. They even eat sandwiches between regular meals (or as they call it, they have brunches and lunches between their regular meals).

The stomach begins to be stuffed with various kinds of foods, and more foods, from the time they awake in the morning until they are asleep at midnight or later. They even eat late at night and early in the morning, if they awake, although they have already eaten two or three heavy meals the previous day. Their stomachs are continually churning and trying to digest a combination of meals.

Then, in addition to eating frequently, they eat nuts of various kinds and candies full of nuts, which the stomach is unable to digest without harming its delicate digestive tract. Trying to digest these various poisonous foods forces the stomach to empty all of its digestive juices, thus causing it to wear out early from hard work.

The loss of our stomachs can cause the loss of our lives. There is a limit to the amount of digestive juice that starts flowing when our food enters our mouths, and continues until it is in the large colon of our body.

Some of the foolish people — when they hear of eating once a day — laugh in fun and scorn and say they cannot live like that. You most certainly cannot live long eating three and four meals a day, and stuffing your body with hog, tough beef, lamb and veal — or any meats.

By nature, the human body was not made to digest meats. Meat causes a great shortening of our lives. We all eat meat. I eat meat also, but it certainly is not good for us. I do not, however, eat pig.

We should not eat any kind of bird. When it actually comes to the best diet for our bodies, no kind of bird should be included except the baby pigeon, called squab, which eats its food from its mother's mouth, after it has been chewed by the mother. Allah (God) has taught me that as soon as the squab is weaned from its mother, and starts eating its own food, we are not to eat it.

No grown pigeons or other birds — not even chickens — are good to eat. Of course, a lot of chickens are raised for the market on corn, oats, and other various types of food, because such food quickly fattens the fowl. When they are raised in the above-mentioned manner, the chickens do not have a chance to eat poisonous food, such as worms, bugs, and filth, which they will do by nature. They will eat anything the hog and the buzzard will eat, if allowed the freedom to do so.

We are, by nature, vegetable and fruit eating people. Bread is also for us to eat. Eat good bread and good fresh vegetables and fruits. Although all of us are not able to eat the right foods, I warn you to stay away from the pig — and I warn you not to eat more than one meal a day. Allah (God), in the Person of Master Fard Muhammad, to Whom praise is due forever, has taught me that we are to wait until we are very hungry before we eat. And, after we eat, we are to wait until we are very hungry before we eat again.

Ninety-five per cent of our sickness comes from eating before we are hungry. Frequent eating puts our stomach to work before it calls for food. Let us eat one meal a day or one meal every two days, as Allah (God) has appointed for us.

God of Right Prescribes Best Foods

We must remember the god of this world (the devil) cannot be taken as a guide for health and life, because he is not such a guide.

We must remember the Biblical prophecy of a God coming to us, whose aim and purpose is to teach the way of life and the prolongation of life, accomplishing these things through the food that we eat (both physically and mentally) and the set times this food should be taken.

The Bible prophesies of His great work of giving to us longer life and the eternal happiness of life without being troubled with the enemy of life and the enemy's effect on life.

The god of this world (the devil) had to try to build a world and teach the people something different from what they had been accustomed to. This is why you see so much change in the way of good to the way of evil.

We must bear in mind that the god of this world was made of the essence of weakness, taught wickedness and trained by a wicked-minded god to destroy the life of the righteous and to change the natural religion of the righteous (the very nature of the righteous), so they would not follow the right course, but follow the wrong course.

He introduced the eating of swine flesh, snakes, reptiles, and all kinds of sea fish that can be considered nothing but scavangers of water, as the hog is a scavenger of the earth. Shrimp, crabs, oysters, catfish, eels (water snakes), and many other species of the water; all types of beans, peas, and nuts were not produced by nature for us to try to use as a diet for our delicate stomachs to digest — not to mention the pig.

The enemy of the righteous has gone to the extreme in everything to shorten, waste, and change the way of right. In trying to make a different world and people from the right world of the original people (Black people), he made a hell for us all.

The foods that the God of righteousness prescribes are the best foods. Let us accept our own (the way Master Fard Muhammad — to whom praise is due forever — has taught us).

We cannot charge the white man with his way of life, and we follow it. If the white man eats poisonous foods and eats three or four times a day, that is his business. We have now learned to distinguish the poisonous food from the non-poisonous. Why should we eat poisonous food? We have learned that eating too often causes us to suffer. So, why should we do so?

Eat one meal a day or one meal every other day, and see how much better you will feel.

There are many different kinds of food that the white man has grown and made. Eat the best of the food that will not destroy your health and bring about a short life. Eat one meal a day and one meal every two days and live.

119

INDEX

INTRODUCING...

THE THREE YEAR ECONOMIC PROGRAM

The **THREE YEAR ECONOMIC PROGRAM** launched by the **Honorable Louis Farrakhan** on October 7, 1991 is designed to address the critical needs of the Black community in the upcoming years.

Your monthly contribution will help to establish farms and businesses that will meet the necessities of life and lay the foundation for our economic survival.

Send your $10 monthly donation to:

THE THREE YEAR ECONOMIC PROGRAM

4855 South Woodlawn Avenue Chicago, Illinois 60615

Muhammad University *of* Islam

7351 South Stony Island Avenue
Chicago, Illinois 60649

SUPPORT
YOUR OWN INDEPENDENT EDUCATIONAL INSTITUTION!

Under the leadership of The Honorable Louis Farrakhan, the Muhammad University of Islam opened to the public on September 6, 1989, including a licensed Early Childhood Learning Center for children ages 2 to 4 years old, and kindergarten to 12th grades. Founded by the Honorable Elijah Muhammad to re-educate our nation into the rich knowledge of self.

We need your financial support to purchase school buses and equipment, and to complete our library and science lab. We acknowledge with deepest gratitude all contributions previously made.

All donations may be mailed to:
**THE HONORABLE ELIJAH MUHAMMAD
EDUCATIONAL FOUNDATION**
c/o Sister Tynetta Muhammad (President)
4855 South Woodlawn Avenue
Chicago, Illinois 60615
MAY ALLAH RICHLY REWARD YOUR EFFORTS

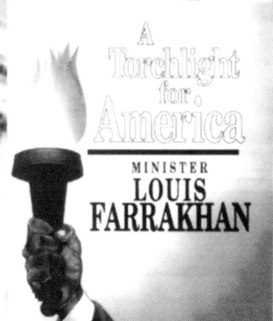

Personally-autographed poster of
Minister Louis Farrakhan

11^{50}

18" X 24"
glossy color

Your contribution helps to further the progress of Minister Farrakhan in continuing the work of The Honorable Elijah Muhammad

Name: _____

Address: _____

City/State/Zip: _____

Make your check or money order payable to:
No. 2 Poor Treasury.
Mail to:
**Minister Louis Farrakhan,
c/o 4855 South Woodlawn Avenue
Chicago, Illinois 60615**

FINAL CALL INC. BOOKS AND TAPES

 ORDER FORM

| Qty | Check One | | | Please Print | Unit Price | Total Price |
	Audio	Video	Book	Title		

SUBTOTAL	
SHIPPING	
TOTAL	

Name_____

Address _____

City/State/Zip _____

Phone _____

Check one: VISA ☐ MASTERCARD ☐ Exp. Date: _____

Please make check or money order payable to : **FINAL CALL** and mail to **FINAL CALL INC.**, 734 W. 79th Street, Chicago Il.,60620. Incude $3.00 for shipping and handling and .50 cents for each additional item. Please allow four weeks for delivery. Wholesale orders are accepted. *Check orders take 14 days before processing; money orders are recommended.*

THE
MUSLIM PROGRAM

What The Muslims Want

This is the question asked most frequently by both the whites and the blacks. The answer to this question I shall state as simply as possible.

1. We want freedom. We want a full and complete freedom.

2. We want justice, Equal justice under the law. We want justice applied equally to all, regardless of creed class or color.

3. We want equality of opportunity. We want equal membership in society with the best in civilized society.

4. We want our people in America whose parents or grandparents were descendants from slaves, to be allowed to establish a separate state or territory of their own-either on this continent or elsewhere. We believe that our former slave masters are obligated to provide such land and that the area must be fertile and minerally rich. We believe that our former slave masters are obligated to maintain and supply our needs in this separate territory for the next 20 to 25 years until we are able to produce and supply our own needs.

Since we cannot get along with them in peace and equality, after giving them 400 years of our sweat and blood receiving in return some of the worst treatment human

beings have ever experienced, we believe our contributions to this land and the suffering forced upon us by white America, justifies our demand for complete separation in a state or territory of our own.

5. We want freedom for all Believers of Islam now held in federal prisons. We want freedom for all black men and women now under death sentence in innumerable prisons in the north as well as in the south.

We want every black man and woman to have the freedom to accept or reject being separated from the slave masters children and establish a land of their own.

We know that the above plan for the solution of the black and white conflict is the best and only answer to the problem between two people.

6. We want an immediate end to the police brutality and mob attacks against the so-called Negro throughout the United States.

We believe that the federal government should intercede to see that black men and women tried in white courts receive justice in accordance with the laws of the land-or allow us to build a new nation for ourselves, dedicated to justice freedom and liberty.

7. As long as we are not allowed to establish a state or territory of our own, we demand not only equal justice under the laws of the United States, but equal employment opportunities-NOW!

We do not believe that after 400 years free or nearly free labor, sweat and blood, which has helped America become rich and powerful, that so many thousands of black people should have to subsist on relief, charity or live in poor houses.

8. We want the government of the United States to exempt our people from ALL taxation as long as we are deprived of equal justice under the laws of the land.

9. We want equal education-but separate schools up to 16 for boys and 18 for girls on the condition the girls be sent to women's colleges and universities. We want all black children educated, taught and trained by their own teachers.

Under such schooling system we believe we will make a better nation of people. The United States government should provide, free, all necessary text books and equipment, schools and college buildings, The Muslim teachers shall be left free to teach and train their people in the way of righteousness, decency and respect.

10. We believe that intermarriage of race mixing should be prohibited. We want the religion of Islam taught without hinderance or supression.

These are some of the things that we, the Muslims, want for our people in North America.

What The Muslims Believe

1. WE BELIEVE in One God whose proper name is Allah.

2. WE BELIEVE in the Holy Qur'an and in the scriptures of all the prophets of God.

3. WE BELIEVE in the truth of the bible, but we believe that it has been tampered with and must be reinterpreted so that mankind will not be snared by the falsehoods that have been added to it.

4. WE BELIEVE in Allah's prophets and the Scriptures they brought to the people.

5. WE BELIEVE in the ressurection of the dead-not in physical resurrection-but mental resurrection. We believe that the so-called Negroes are most in need of mental resurrection; therefore, they will be resurrected first. Furthermore, we believe we are the people of God's choice, as it has been written, that God would choose the rejected and the despised. We can find no other persons fitting this description in these last days more than the so-called Negroes in America. We believe in the resurrection of the righteous.

6. WE BELIEVE in the judgement; we believe this first judgement will take place as God revealed, in America...

7. WE BELIEVE this is the time in history for the separation of the so-called Negroes and the so-called white Americans. We be-

lieve the black man should be freed in name as well as in fact. By this we meanthat he should be freed from the name imposed upon him by his former slave masters. Names which identified him as being the slave masters slave. We believe that if we are free indeed, we should go in our own people names the black people of the earth.

8. WE BELIEVE in justice for all, whether in God or not; we believe as others, that we are due equal justice as human beings.We believe in equality-as a nation of equals.We do not believe that we are equal with our slave masters in the status of "freed slaves".

We recognize and respect American citizens as independent peoples and we respect their laws which govern this nation.

9. WE BELIEVE that the offer of intergration is hypocritcal and is made by those who are trying to deceive the Black peoples into believing that their 400 year-old openenemies of freedom, justice and equality are, all of a sudden, their " friends". Furthermore, we believe that such deception is intended to prevent Black people from realizing that the time in history has arrived for the separation from the whites of this nation.

If the white people are truthful about their professed freindship toward the so-called Negro, they can prove it by dividing up America with

their slaves.

We do not believe that America will be able to furnish enough jobs for her own millions of unemployed, in addition to jobs for the 20,000,000 Black people as well.

10. WE BELIEVE that we who declare ourselves to be righteous Muslims, should not participate in wars which take the lives of humans. We do not believe this nation should force us to take part in such wars, for we have nothing to gain from it unless America agrees to give us the necessary territory wherein we may have something to fight for.

11. WE BELIEVE our women should be respected and protected as the women of other nationalities are respected and protected.

12. WE BELIEVE that Allah (God) appeared in the Person of Master W. Fard Muhammad, July, 1930; the long-awaited "Messiah" of the Christians and the "Mahdi" of the Muslims.

We believe further and lastly that Allah is God and besides HIM there is no God and He will bring about a universal government of peace wherein we all can live in peace together.